THEY WENT ANOTHER WAY

THEY WENT ANOTHER WAY

A Hollywood Memoir

BRUCE ERIC KAPLAN

Henry Holt and Company

New York

Henry Holt and Company
Publishers since 1866
120 Broadway
New York, New York 10271
www.henryholt.com

Henry Holt and 🅗 are registered trademarks of Macmillan Publishing Group, LLC.

Lyrics from "In Our Time" © 2014 Hamilton Leithauser

Library of Congress Cataloging-in-Publication Data

Names: Kaplan, Bruce Eric, author.
Title: They went another way : a Hollywood memoir / Bruce Eric Kaplan.
Description: First edition. | New York : Henry Holt and Company, 2024.
Identifiers: LCCN 2024017054 | ISBN 9781250370334 (hardcover) |
    ISBN 9781250370327 (ebook)
Subjects: LCSH: Kaplan, Bruce Eric, author. | Authors, American—20th
    century—Biography. | Authors, American—21st century—Biography. |
    Cartoonists—United States—Biography. | Screenwriters—United
    States—Biography. | LCGFT: Autobiographies.
Classification: LCC PS3561.A5534 Z46 2024 | DDC 813/.52 [B]—dc23/
    eng/20240521
LC record available at https://lccn.loc.gov/2024017054

Our books may be purchased in bulk for promotional, educational, or business use.
Please contact your local bookseller or the Macmillan Corporate and Premium Sales
Department at (800) 221-7945, extension 5442, or by email at
MacmillanSpecialMarkets@macmillan.com.

First Edition 2024

Designed by Gabriel Guma

Printed in the United States of America

10 9 8 7 6 5 4 3 2 1

This book is dedicated to Kate, Henry, and Eve, and all the other kind (and unkind) people who didn't ask to be in this book.

JANUARY 10, 2022

I'm looking to have a profound experience, I thought to myself a couple of days ago as I woke up from a dream in the middle of the night. It was almost as if that was the last sentence I said in the dream. But I am getting ahead of myself.

First, I want to tell you that I am starting this journal to keep from going mad. I used to say that the cartoons were my journals, but now that I don't draw cartoons anymore, I am acutely feeling the loss of a way to express how I feel and what I am thinking about.

I want to have a record of this time in my life for a variety of reasons, which I am still trying to understand and articulate to myself.

Five years ago I wrote a television pilot for Sony about a woman who starts a relationship with a man half her age. They meet when he is in prison and she starts writing in letters to him. They fall in love, and when he unexpectedly gets let out of prison, she is forced to see if they can have a relationship in real life, which upsets those around her, and herself, actually. It is sort of my version of *Harold and Maude*, but it also has a *Moonstruck* quality. It never had a good title and it never went out into the world because I believe Sony felt it was a little "soft."

A year ago, my new agents at Creative Artists Agency (CAA), Rob and Laura, started sending it to actresses. In August, they said Glenn Close had read it and wanted to do it, and we had a meeting. She went off to shoot something and my agents and, mostly, my manager, Ellyn, spent all fall getting Sony to agree to being a "silent" partner, as they were the ones who paid me for it and still had rights to it.

In December, after Sony agreed it was ours, Glenn wanted to attach a director. I heard she wanted to send it to Ron Howard. I said that was fine with me.

"You can't have Ron Howard direct this," my friend Gary said when I told him.

"He'll never want to do it," I said. "It's fine."

A few days later, we heard that he was passing because he "didn't connect with the material."

"I'm sure he didn't," I said to Ellyn. "I've never connected to his material. We don't have any overlap."

Then it was the holidays and then people were getting back from the holidays and now I am supposedly going to have a meeting with Glenn Close and a director named Max something—I can never remember his name. He directed *Palm Springs* and a movie with Glenn that they just finished and hasn't come out yet.

The reason I say I am supposedly having a meeting, instead of having a meeting, is that three days ago, my agent's assistant asked me if I could Zoom with them on January eighteenth or twentieth. I said either would work. And now I am waiting for Glenn to confirm one of those days. I assume nothing at this point. If you told me today that this meeting would never happen, I would believe you.

Earlier today the Phil Collins song that was in *Against All Odds* popped into my head, and I had a sense memory of being in my body when that song would come on the radio when I was in college. I miss being in that body and being the person I was then, who assumed things would happen.

When I woke up in the middle of the night two nights ago and had that thought about a profound experience, it felt very meaningful. I thought, I have to say that in my meeting with Glenn and

Max, if there is an actual meeting. So I emailed it to myself so I wouldn't forget it in the morning:

> Sat, Jan 8, 2:21 AM (2 days ago) to me
>
> Subj: GLENN AND MAX
>
> Im looking to have a profound experience.
> Sent from my iPhone

Now, of course, it doesn't seem at all meaningful to me and I feel they might think it odd if I do say it. I have literally no idea why I thought this was so compelling. Maybe I miss the person who I was two nights ago too.

JANUARY 11

Glenn confirmed the meeting with Max and myself a week from today. I now have to reread the script and come up with something to say. I did the same thing six months ago when I first met with Glenn. I wrote down all these new ideas about subsequent episodes, and now I can't find the piece of paper and have no idea what I said to her. Maybe she will know.

I woke up agitated this morning, as has been happening to me more often than not in the last few months. I haven't had a job in over half a year, and that has not been fun. But more to the point, the world itself has become so agitating. It feels like it is all coming apart. I read an article that said the United States is already in a civil war and we are all just walking around ignoring it. It feels like things are going to get worse before they get better, or *if* they get better, I suppose.

I was driving home from dropping Henry off at his high school and I thought, How can I make myself feel better? I meditate first thing when I wake up and then do "morning pages," and sometimes that makes me feel better. But not today. So now what was I to do?

I thought of how an old friend, I will call her Liz, is no longer in my life. For over two decades, she was a big presence for me. I met her when I was a teenager, then became friends with her later when we worked together as assistants when I was in my early twenties. She was often upset, constantly crying. I believe she cried the first day we worked together. But she also liked to laugh. And we did have fun.

But as the years and years passed, I stopped having fun with her. She was just upset all the time and complained about the same things over and over and over again. She would ask for advice and never take it. Above all, she blamed the entire world for her problems, which was challenging to hear each time I would see her.

As anyone in their right mind knows, we are our problems. The only solution is for us to do something different.

"I just can't do this anymore," I said to Kate after one night where Liz sat on our couch and complained and cried for two hours.

"You have to," Kate said. "There's no way out."

Then, miraculously, one day the telephone rang. It was Liz, and she was mad at me. She cried and said I hadn't called her a few days before, after something I felt didn't warrant me checking in on her.

"You're a bad friend," she said.

I was shocked. For years and years I had been what I considered to be "there for her" whenever she needed it, which was a lot. So to be called a bad friend was unnerving.

"Oh," I said calmly. "If you feel that way, then you shouldn't have me in your life." And shortly after, I ended the conversation.

And that was that. We never spoke again. Magically, I was given an out. I am smiling happily as I type this. So today, when I was anxious and upset about the world, I thought, well, at least I don't have Liz in my life. It gives me the biggest lift. It makes me feel like magic can still happen.

But now, years later, I realize in a way she was right. I had stopped being the person she needed me to be. I was too exhausted. Today, I am only filled with love for her and am grateful to her for the good times we had. Liz was doing her best. We are all doing our best, even when it doesn't look that way. And I wish good things for her, and hope she has found some peace.

JANUARY 12

Now Glenn wants to have a premeeting before our meeting with Max. I said of course, but haven't heard what day it will be. I have been preparing for the meeting by putting down thoughts on future episodes, season arcs, that type of thing.

It's a little strange to be coming up with ideas for an aspirational comedy along the lines of a Nancy Meyers movie while living in such dystopian times. Los Angeles is still desolate with closed businesses, off-the-grid people walking into traffic, everyone in masks, each person in sight staring into their phones, etc.

In my first meeting with Glenn six months ago, I brought up the cognitive dissonance of coming up with ideas for this show when everything is so depressing at the moment.

"The show's about hope," she said. "I'm only interested in watching things about hope."

"I know," I said. "I wrote that down in my notes today. Hope, faith, magic, beauty. I know it's about all those things. But it just feels weird to be working on something that is so disconnected from our current reality."

For almost all my writing and drawing career, I have worked on things that have been drawn from current reality. And that is not the case here. This is more drawn from how things used to be, or how they may be again, or most likely, how things should be but never really can be anymore.

Last night, Henry was in his room, and as I walked by I heard him practicing a new song on his guitar. It was "Rhiannon" by Fleetwood Mac. Honestly, that moment of walking by his room was one of the greatest moments of my life.

Over ten years ago, I was asked to be a "Guest DJ" on KCRW. It was more of an interview than actually being a DJ. They asked creative types, I assume, to come up with five songs that inspire them. All the songs I chose were from the 1970s because I had just been writing a screenplay that took place in the 1970s that featured the music of the era. My fifth song was "Rhiannon." Here is what I said:

BEK: "Rhiannon." The reason that I included this song is that I don't know why I included this song, but let me explain.

I do have this association with this song, and it's that I was a teenager, and I was driving on South Orange Avenue in probably Livingston, New Jersey, and I was very upset and I remember hearing this song, and it sort of provided a landscape for my upsetness. And was soothing. And it gave a grandioseness to my upsetness, which is a great thing art can do, make whatever thing that you're feeling feel more epic.

Song: Fleetwood Mac—"Rhiannon"

BEK: I don't know if it really inspired me, but, stepping back, I knew I had to include that song for "one of the five songs that inspired you," but I don't know exactly why, and I feel like that's a really important thing in terms of being creative, like to listen to a higher voice, be true to one's creative self, even if there's no very strong, easily articulated reason.

There's something connected to my unconscious with this song, and I just don't have the key yet. Again, it's like a big part of the creative process. Your job is to delve into it to figure out why you're connecting with something.

Now I am sitting here, trying to figure out why hearing Henry play "Rhiannon" last night was so meaningful for me. I think it is that I never could have predicted it, or any of my life. When I was a teenager in New Jersey listening to that song and having those feelings driving down South Orange Avenue, I never could have imagined that I would thirty years later be talking about it on a radio station in Los Angeles and then forty years later, hearing my son sing it as he played it on the guitar. It is almost as if the moment proved to me that there is magic in this world. I mean, I know there is nothing really magical about it, but it feels magical, so it is magical.

Maybe it is the interplay of the distance between the moments and the continuity of the moments that is the true magic. Maybe it is particularly magical because it is happening at a time where truth and beauty and art seem almost impossible, and yet it shows that it still is possible.

One thing I remembered about an hour ago when I was thinking about all this as I was washing dishes is that I had a terrible car accident on South Orange Avenue not that long after the "Rhiannon" moment. There was, and I assume still is, a particularly curvy part of South Orange Avenue. It was called the S's because it was so curvy. There were tons of guardrails on the curves, and most of them were dented or mangled in some way because so many people had accidents on the S's.

One rainy night I was one of those people. I was going too fast, and the road was slippery. I was driving three of my friends somewhere, maybe to Don's, an awful restaurant that I would kill to eat at right now if it still existed. Anyway, the car skidded off the road and I believe turned completely over and landed upside down near a tree. The car was totaled, but all of us just got out of the car, not one person was hurt. I have no memory of how I got home, but I assume the police just came and took each of us home. And then I guess my parents got a new car.

Clearly, that night could have gone a lot differently. One or all of us could have died. If I had died that night, I obviously wouldn't have gone on KCRW and, of course, Henry wouldn't exist.

And maybe that is the most magical part of all. It's just that Henry exists. Although to be exact, the first miracle is that Kate exists, then Henry, then our daughter, Eve, who sadly came up with the awful idea of going to boarding school this year.

JANUARY 13

It's Thursday. Glenn still hasn't set a day or time to meet before we have our meeting with Max on Tuesday.

I took a walk with my friend Max (I have about a dozen Maxes in my life) in Roxbury Park in Beverly Hills yesterday. Max lives a block away from the park. On that block, he pointed out an enormous Let's Go Brandon sign in a first-floor apartment window. It was truly terrifying. It's like we are living in Germany in the 1930s.

"Did you see the Bob Einstein documentary?" he asked me as we walked around the park.

"No," I said. "I knew his wife, Roberta, years ago and met him a few times and never liked him."

I explained that I met Roberta through Carol Matthau. Carol was married to Walter Matthau, but had been married to William Saroyan and been friends with Truman Capote and a million other interesting people. I had a job helping Carol write her memoir, and Roberta worked at Tiffany's, which was Carol's favorite store in the world.

Carol talked to Roberta on the telephone often and went to see her at Tiffany's often. I am not sure what Carol bought for herself at Tiffany's, but I am assuming it was jewelry.

I do know that there was a small room in Carol's house next to her bedroom. She showed it to me one day, and in it were hundreds of small boxes, many of which came from Tiffany's.

"This is my gift closet," she said, as if people always had gift closets in their houses. Maybe certain people did, but I didn't know them. Or maybe Carol was the only one.

She took a small blue box from Tiffany's and gave it to me. In it was a small silver frame and little cardboard-like squares of parchment inside it to use as a calendar. I kept it on my desk for years, but once I stopped having a desk, I stopped having the Tiffany's calendar.

During the year and a half I worked for Carol, I sometimes went to see Roberta at Tiffany's in Beverly Hills and picked up things for Carol, or returned things for her.

Even after I stopped working for Carol, I would still go to Tiffany's occasionally. She gave me a clock from Tiffany's, which also sat on my desk for years. When the battery would die, I would just go to Tiffany's and I would be given a new battery at no charge. I wonder if they still do that.

It doesn't seem possible that Carol's gift closet could exist in the same world as Let's Go Brandon signs, and I guess it doesn't.

Yesterday, my old friend Jen texted me that Joyce Eliason had died. She was someone thirty years older than me who I knew in my twenties. Jen knew her through me and Jen now texted me various memories of things Joyce had said that stayed with her all these years.

I texted Jen back:

It's like she left pieces of herself with you. And she
has/had no idea
It's very moving

Jen answered:

Yes it is

Later in the day yesterday, I found not one but two dead birds outside our house, one in the front and one in the back, both seeming to have flown into the large glass windows of our living room.

It happens occasionally, but never two on the same day before. It was actually frightening in a strange way.

Today, I went into the backyard and was overjoyed not to find a dead bird.

That was going to be my last line for today, but then something just happened that makes me have to continue writing.

I was planning to leave something that happened yesterday out of the story, but now I can't.

Before I found the two dead birds, I was returning from dropping Henry off at school and saw one very still bird sitting on the ground. It was a quite unusual sight. The bird seemed to maybe be breathing but on the other hand was also unnaturally still. This was before I found the two dead birds, mind you. I went inside and told Kate about it.

"I think it's dead," I said.

"Don't do anything yet," she said, as I am the person in the house who gets rid of dead birds.

"Okay," I said.

I went back a few minutes later and it was still there. "It has to be dead," I said.

"Just give it time," Kate said.

I went back a few minutes later and the bird was gone.

"You were right," I said. I looked at the cement where the bird had been sitting, and there was a tiny dark bowel movement.

"I guess it was just constipated," I said. "But shouldn't the bowel movement be white, like what shows up on cars?"

"Maybe that's urine," Kate said.

"That can't be urine," I said. "How could urine look like that?"

And that was that. Until an hour later when I saw another bird on the cement outside our front door sitting unnaturally.

"There's another one," I said to Kate.

"That's creepy," she said. "It's very apocalyptic."

I checked on the bird a few minutes later. It was in the same position. And then a few minutes later, it was gone, and there was another small dark bowel movement.

At the end of the day, I came back from picking up Henry and that is when I found the two dead birds. I was so unnerved that I accidentally broke the sliding screen door a few feet away from the dead bird in the backyard.

I agitatedly cleaned up the birds and put them in the garbage and then took a walk with Kate.

"What does it mean?" I asked.

"I don't know," she said.

The reason I am telling you all this is just now, I found another still bird sitting on the cement out front. It was there for a few minutes, then it left another strange bowel movement.

I was going to leave out the two constipated birds because it seemed too confusing. But now that there is a third one today, it feels like I have to tell the whole story.

Which is all to say, every story has something left out of it, and this one almost had the two constipated birds from yesterday left out of it.

JANUARY 14

Yesterday afternoon, I got an email saying Glenn wanted to talk today, so we are set for a Zoom at five. I am going to pitch the idea of shooting in Canada, as a way to escape the insanity of this country.

I had a terrible night's sleep, so I will look awful for my Zoom.

I once dated a woman and whenever she told her mother that she was going to do something like go out to dinner with someone or go to a party, her mother would loudly say in a southern sing-song, "Look pretty! Look pretty!"

I wish it could be that simple for me, but I feel like there is no hope of me looking pretty today.

I remember my girlfriend telling me that once, when she and her siblings were little, her mother was so depressed that she decided to paint the entire house black.

I found that sort of admirable. I like bold statements. I think we need more people taking things to the next level, even if it's the next level of depression.

Her mother was seemingly still depressed when we were dating. She spent most days lying in a small dark bedroom on the first floor of a big house in Bel Air and only left the house occasionally to go to Neiman Marcus or to church.

Periodically, she would be in a lot of pain. Apparently, she would get abnormally long hemorrhoids caused by lying in bed all day, and then would refuse to have a doctor take care of them, until the pain got too much to bear. You never hear about hemorrhoids anymore. Maybe they went away.

There were many, many commercials for hemorrhoid creams when I was a kid, which now seems hard to imagine. All day long you would hear about hemorrhoid creams and now you never do.

That girlfriend and I had our first kiss in the parking lot of Ships

Coffee Shop on La Cienega Boulevard, which I think is the most perfect place in the world to have a first kiss. At first, I thought it was at Norms, but now I remember it was at Ships.

Norms still exists, but Ships is gone forever. So I guess it *was* the most perfect place in the world to have had a first kiss there, since no one will again.

JANUARY 15

There was another dead bird today. I'm waiting to clean it up in case another one shows up. It's the type of thing you really only want to do once in a day, not twice, because it's a laborious process involving getting the rake and using it to put the bird in a paper bag, then throwing it out in the trash.

While Eve is at school, I have been using her room, my old office, as a place for my Zoom meetings, and before my meeting with Glenn yesterday I lay down for twenty minutes on Eve's bed with green tea bags on my eyes, listening to aura-cleansing music on YouTube. "Look pretty! Look pretty!" I heard in my head.

I am not sure if I looked pretty for the meeting, but I think there was definite improvement from how I looked before the green tea bags and cleansed aura.

The meeting with Glenn went well. Her manager Christian joined us. Glenn was very unpretentious and straightforward. In the middle of the meeting, I thought, I like her. She has a nice hearty New Englander quality.

At the end of the hour, I talked about how I view this project like activism almost. The world is so ugly at the moment. This show is hopefully about finding truth and beauty and joy in the world despite all signs of them not being there.

When I was coming up with storylines for Glenn's character yesterday, I wrote down something about her going to see Broadway musicals year in and year out, yet never having enjoyed one since *A Chorus Line* in 1975 or whenever it was. Glenn's love interest reacts with disbelief.

"That's almost fifty years of not liking whatever musical you were seeing," he says. "Why do you keep going?"

"Hope," she said. "I guess."

In case you haven't guessed, this comes from my own experience. I bring it up in this moment because to me, there is something uniquely truthful and joyous and beautiful about *A Chorus Line*. I wish everything were like it, or at least one other thing.

It's the end of the day. I just checked outside. No additional dead birds. So I'm getting a paper bag and the rake and throwing this one out.

JANUARY 16

Today I had a day riddled with fear about what it means to live in a country where one political party is against voting rights.

Also, I was cleaning my daughter's room and saw a pair of sunglasses caught in a half-shut drawer. When I opened the drawer to get the sunglasses out and put them in fully, I saw in the rest of the drawer dozens and dozens of ChapSticks. Who would want to save old ChapSticks and why are people so mysterious?

JANUARY 17

I meet again with Glenn and Max tomorrow morning at nine o'clock. Yesterday, I got an email from Evan, a producer I am

THEY WENT ANOTHER WAY

working with on another idea I have. It's for a show about some Americans in New Zealand. He said he told Will Forte about the show, and Will is interested in having a meeting about being the lead. That is to be scheduled for probably the week after next, which usually means sometime after the week after next.

I just realized this book is like *Monster* by John Gregory Dunne, one of my favorite books to reread. I have a very small group of books that I reread, and all the other ones are by either Nora Ephron, Delia Ephron, or one by their father, Henry Ephron. *Monster* is about his and Joan Didion's experience writing *Up Close and Personal*, a supposedly bad movie I have never seen. I am so excited that I now have my Monster, but I am not sure yet what my Monster will be or even if I really do have my Monster. My Monster could be about me never even getting to have my Monster.

I just paused and cleaned the toilet. I don't know why this toilet gets so dirty so quickly. Of all the toilets I have cleaned in my life, it's as if this one is the dirtiest. It feels as if it makes itself dirty when no one is even using it. I just had a sad thought—what if this book ends up about me cleaning the toilet all year? It's definitely possible.

Now "Solace" by Scott Joplin is playing on the radio. It always makes me think of *The Sting*, which I saw as a kid at the Strand movie theater in Summit, New Jersey.

The line for *The Sting* was the longest line for a movie that I had ever seen. It went out the front of the Strand, then around the side of the Strand, and then around the back of the Strand. It just kept going and going and going. Finally, we got to the end of the line. It didn't seem possible for the movie theater to hold this many people. The line was very slow, so slow that by the time we got inside the theater, the movie had been playing for twenty minutes.

When the lights came up at the end, my family got up to go. "We didn't see the first twenty minutes," I said.

"So?" one of my brothers probably said.

"So we should stay to watch the first twenty minutes," I said, in disbelief that anyone would think otherwise.

Everyone else said we should just leave.

"I'm not going," I said. I was nine, the youngest member of the family, but also the firmest. There was no way I was leaving that theater.

And we stayed, watched the first twenty minutes of the movie, and then went home. Everything always comes back to setting one's intention firmly so that the world has to yield to it. So I am learning from my younger self and refusing to have a toilet year.

Instead, I am setting my intention firmly with these Glenn Close and Will Forte shows. Let's see how I do.

JANUARY 18

Someone ate a lot of our bushes last night. There are five bushes in the backyard that are gone. Yesterday, I found some excrement of unknown origins in the backyard and sadly cleaned it up. Maybe that same individual came back at night and ate our bushes.

I signed onto Zoom at nine for my meeting. Only Max was there. I introduced myself and Max and I talked for a while. Then we got emails that Glenn was unable to sign on. So then I had a Zoom at ten with Max, Glenn, and Christian. I love Max's ideas, and we ended the meeting all agreeing to go out into the world together, with all three of us having the same goal of ending up at HBO or maybe HBO Max.

At one point in the second meeting, we talked about making the decision to be happy. I referenced *Man's Search for Meaning* by Viktor E. Frankl, which isn't perhaps exactly about that. But it is related in that he figures out how to survive in a concentration camp by focusing on his love for his wife and his life after the camp if he gets to have a life after the camp. At least that is what my memory of it is. It obviously could be completely different.

It seems relevant today in that it is so hard to not get bogged down in the fear of what the world is turning into. As Glenn said, it is not about pretending the ugliness isn't happening. It is about figuring out how to be in touch with hope and art and beauty, which are still real too. Or can be again.

I keep thinking about my missing bushes. Now that they are gone, I realize I really took them for granted. They were ordinary bushes, not really that special, which I hate to say about them now that they are gone. But maybe they actually were special, just quietly special. I just didn't know. The bottoms of each one are still there, so I hope that means they will grow again.

I have spent so much time during the last two years being in the backyard and looking at all the more overtly dramatic plants and thinking about how lucky I was to be looking at them. But now I know I am lucky for all that is out there, not just the flashier foliage.

I feel like Dorothy at the end of *The Wizard of Oz*. The bushes are my Auntie Em. If they do come back, I am going to cry and throw my arms around them like Dorothy does to Auntie Em at the end of the movie.

JANUARY 19

I read the news this morning and was filled with dread for the future. Then I went to the Arts section and read an interview with Kathy Griffin. It was so long, but somehow I finished it. Then I read an interview with Lena Dunham in the *Hollywood Reporter*. I hadn't gone looking for it, but it came into my Twitter feed, and for some reason I clicked on it. Somehow it all just ate at my brain, and now I have no thoughts.

The Kathy and Lena interviews made me think about how we

all have a version of ourselves that some people may agree with and other people may not agree with. What if we were all open to our version of ourselves not always being the most real version of who we are? In this moment, I would like to have a version of myself different from the one that is in my head.

My manager, Ellyn, called me yesterday and asked how I felt about the comedians Kate Berlant and John Early.

"I love them," I said. She explained that they have two ideas for a TV show and wanted to run them by me to see if I would supervise them. Maybe they are my destiny, not Glenn.

JANUARY 20

Late in the day yesterday, Ellyn called me again to say that Kate and John were also going to be meeting with another writer.

"Do you still want to have the meeting?" she asked.

"I'm fine either way," I said. "What do you think I should do?"

"My first reaction is 'F' them," she said. "But I am not sure."

"I would like to know the name of the writer," I said.

"That's what I think too. It might be someone like Gary," she said, referring to my friend Gary. It would be odd for me and him to both meet with Kate and John.

We hung up and she came back with the name of the other writer. It is actually a friend of Gary's, but not Gary.

"I know him, but we're not friends," I wrote in an email. "I'm fine to meet with them."

I was a little sad, though. I was hoping my competition would be someone a little more interesting than this person.

There has been silence from Glenn's team for the past two days. I am starting to feel like there might be a glitch.

Something that happened almost twenty years ago popped into my head this morning, I'm not sure why.

I was in the writers' room for a TV show and someone, I believe it was me, was talking about someone and said, "There's something a little off about him."

One of the other writers glared at me.

"I hate when someone says that," she said angrily.

"Why?" I asked, genuinely confused.

She launched into a long tirade about how wrong it was to say there was something a little off about someone. I think her point was it wasn't fair to say something negative about someone in such an abstract way. It sort of minimizes the person you are talking about. And I do think she had a point.

However, as she went on and on and on, I realized something seemed really off about her. And I wondered if she knew that about herself and that was why she was so angry.

A production assistant from the show I worked on last year in New Zealand just emailed me. He is a writer looking for advice. Here is what he wrote:

> I think something I'm struggling with at the moment is now that more people are reading and giving notes, I'm having to either stand up for ideas I believe in or compromise.
>
> Especially with jokes. There feels like a disconnect between what I find funny to what the "big-wigs" reading the drafts laugh at. How do you find the note process? Did you always know instinctively what was and what wasn't going to work for your stories? How do you deal with burnout? Did you ever get tired? Writing used to really energize me but lately, its been a mixed bag.

Here is what I wrote back:

Hmm.

These are my answers, although of course, I may not be addressing exactly what you are asking.

Re: jokes, I had confusion early on when I was writing in that I tried hard to make something "funny" and would often fail.

Now I strictly write what makes me laugh, not what I think someone else would think is funny, and that has made all the difference for me. It is a much more enjoyable and honest way to approach what I am writing.

I find the note process different from project to project, depending on who is giving the notes. In general, I much prefer getting notes from other writers than from anyone else, as they tend to give notes that make the script more what it wants to be, not less what it wants to be.

At this exact moment in time, I do know instinctively what is going to work for my stories. Although I would not use that phrasing. For me, I follow what the characters/stories want to be. They lead me and if I start to push them in a way they don't want to go, then I go back a step and listen to them tell me where they do want to go.

Re burnout, I don't really get burned out when I am fully engaged with a script. I do get tired of having to generate "documents" for executives saying what a script is going to be. But if I am actually writing a script, then it tends to relax me, as it is very pleasant to get lost in another world, especially as this world in the United States gets more and more nightmarish.

I just reread his first question and I see I didn't really answer it that well, but I am not sure how to answer it better.

JANUARY 21

Okay, I just had my meeting with Kate Berlant and John Early. There weren't two ideas. There was just one, which they talked me through, and I said I would be happy to supervise them if they wanted. I question how easy it would be to sell this idea, but what do I know? I really like them both, but at the same time, they are nerve-racking for me. I am too porous, and when I talk to them, I feel whatever is happening for them too much.

I got an email that Glenn's and Max's agents spoke to my lawyer to get a fuller understanding of Sony's role in the project, and everyone is comfortable. So now Max's agent just has to confirm with Max that he is on board, then we decide next steps.

A friend of ours had surgery to remove something cancerous a few months ago. Yesterday, Kate said she talked to her, and there is a chance for recurrence. Her husband has been urging her to add turmeric and green tea to her diet. So last night, instead of making cabbage the way I usually do, I looked for a recipe with turmeric. This is what I found on a website called Food and Wine:

INGREDIENTS
- 2 tablespoons extra-virgin olive oil
- 1 1/2 teaspoons cumin seeds

- 3 pounds green cabbage, cored and thinly shredded
- 1 1/2 teaspoons turmeric
- 1/2 teaspoons kosher salt

DIRECTIONS

1. In a large saucepan, heat the olive oil over moderate heat. Stir in the cumin seeds and cook until they are fragrant, about 30 seconds.
2. Add the shredded cabbage, turmeric, and kosher salt and cook, stirring occasionally, until the cabbage is softened and browned in spots, 15 to 20 minutes.

Serve hot.

I liked it. But you don't need as much salt as they think you do.

After dinner (and after a few glasses of wine), I shoved tons of flavor-blasted Goldfish into my mouth, which probably undid all the good the one and a half teaspoons of turmeric did.

In the car ride home from school, "Thunder Road" came up on Henry's Spotify list.

"Ech," I said.

"Do you want me to change it?" he asked.

"I'm fine to listen if you like it," I said.

"I hate Bruce Springsteen," he said.

"I didn't think it was possible for me to love you any more than I did already," I said. "But now I do."

JANUARY 22

I spent a lot of time screaming in my car today.

JANUARY 23

I am having a day where very lawless people have disregarded rules and done what they wanted instead, especially dog owners. I was very calm and decided just to observe things, not be so reactive.

I also got a lot of toothpaste all over myself in the morning. About midafternoon, it became a screaming-in-the-car day again.

JANUARY 24

It's a Monday morning. I am waiting to hear if Max Barbakow is officially in for the Glenn Close script. I am waiting to hear if Kate Berlant and John Early picked me or the other person. I am waiting to hear when I am going to meet with Will Forte about my New Zealand show. And I am actually waiting on several other things I don't feel like typing about.

My friend Beth Lapides once told me about all the things she was waiting to hear back about.

"Well, you're good at waiting," I told her, which she loved for some reason.

Kate had mysterious red marks on her face, and her dermatologist did some tests and ascertained it's rosacea. Apparently, rosacea can be caused by the sun or the wind or eating beans or a million other things. So anything in the entire world can cause rosacea.

3:13 P.M.

I have now heard from Christian, Glenn's manager. He sent a group email to me and Glenn saying we are all officially moving forward and will have a call later this week to talk about a timeline. It is fun to have Glenn Close's email address.

It was a very disturbing news day like every news day seems

to be now. One article seemed to indicate a future civil war in the United States is now more likely than not. It's such a strange time to try to be creative yet also be connected to reality.

Everyone I know is talking about where they should move to, when they should move to this place, oh, there's nowhere to move to, help.

4:28 P.M.

I just spent almost an hour making the worst spinach yogurt dip.

JANUARY 25

Once when I was a kid, my older brother Michael and my father were having a fight in the kitchen. Then Michael ran out of the house and got in his car in the driveway. Suddenly, we heard a loud crash. Michael ran back in and came into the kitchen.

"Why didn't you tell me you were parked behind me?" he yelled at my father.

I don't know why I thought about it this morning. But it still brings a smile to my face fifty years later.

Two men are in the house as I write this, working on our heating unit, if that is what it is called. Everything has been breaking lately, then when someone comes to fix it, they say we can't fix it, we need to come back to fix it. So this is the day they came back to fix it.

I haven't written a script since last April or May. That's a long time for me. I wish I had a script to write today. When I get lost in writing, the day just disappears, which is the greatest feeling in the world. I wish the day would disappear today.

I just spoke to the heating repair people. There is a problem. They are supposed to be replacing an air handler, but the new air handler they brought is too big. So it seems like they are going to leave today again not having solved the heating problem. It all feels very of this time. Someone comes to fix things, they try to fix things, they then can't fix things, and they say they will need to come back in the future to hopefully fix things.

11:52 A.M.

I was folding clothes and practicing mindfulness, just fully being in the moment. It made me notice how beautiful the sunlight was and how peaceful it was in our bedroom. There was just the slightest sound of the folded clothes being put on the bed. It was only for a few moments, but it was such a nice respite from the turmoil in my brain.

JANUARY 26

The heating repair men are back today. They found a smaller air handler and are now putting it in. So sometimes things still do happen.

I woke up in the middle of the night, feeling an enormous weight on my chest.

I can't do this anymore, I thought. I can't keep waiting and waiting for something to happen.

"I want to start my own business," I said to Kate as she was making her coffee in the morning.

She gave me a strange look, as if to say, are you out of your mind?

"Eric started his own business," I said, referencing our neighbor who was a CFO for a film company before he got laid off a few years ago.

"Eric's a money person," Kate said.

"Well, Ben started his own business," I said. Ben is someone else we know who was a network executive then got fired a few years ago and now has some new venture, which I was told about a few months ago from another friend, but it completely disinterested me, so I promptly forgot what it was. "Ben seems like he was just some liberal arts person."

Kate looked at me, not fully convinced. "What's your idea?" she asked.

"I don't know."

She was silent for a moment. We just looked at each other.

"I don't want to be a naysayer," she finally said, with a big "But . . ." unsaid at the end.

I sighed.

"It's fine," I said. "You can be a naysayer." Starting my own business was starting to seem like less of a realistic solution than it had in the middle of the night.

I emailed my agents and manager, asking when we are going to have this call with everyone about next steps on the Glenn Close project.

Laura from CAA immediately emailed back that she and Rob are still waiting to hear back from Max's agent that Max is officially on board.

I responded that I just assumed he already was, since how can it be taking six days for Max's agent to talk to him?

I keep finding new places in the house to clean to make the waiting go by faster. Sadly, one of the new places is the oven, which I always forget to clean. I should clean it more often.

10:10 A.M.

The heating repair people just said they can't put in the new air handler because it would require removing a panel with a nail finish gun, which they don't have, and they don't want to permanently damage the panel.

So ... they are leaving. And I texted the people who put in the panel five years ago to see if they could come back to remove it so that the heating repair can then come back. And then after that, the nail finish gun people could come back to reinstall the panel.

So at the moment it does feel like nothing will happen with anything. I wrote a line in a pilot years ago where one character says, "I don't need progress. I just need the illusion of progress." It feels in this moment like it's not even possible anymore to get the illusion of progress.

On the way to school this morning, Henry's Spotify recommended we listen to the instrumental version of "Moon River" from *Breakfast at Tiffany's*. As it played, I was taken back to when I first saw the movie on television when I was a kid. It would play on I think ABC or maybe NBC (but definitely not CBS) in prime time once or twice a year. I was so happy when it would come on. It was fun and stylish and, above all, beautiful to look at. But there was more than that.

Oh, this is love, I thought as I watched it. It really defined love in a way that other movies or TV shows didn't.

When I worked for Carol Matthau, she talked about being a kid and having a similar reaction to *Wuthering Heights*, but I never liked *Wuthering Heights* that much, and it certainly didn't explain love to me. Heathcliff and Catherine seemed like stunted and stiff dolls engaged in a lot of projection on each other. Not that I knew what projection was then, but in a way I did.

In *Breakfast at Tiffany's*, the George Peppard and Audrey Hepburn characters seemed to really see each other and accept each other wholly as they were or as they aspired to be. It was very profound to watch.

The only bad part about the movie was the Mickey Rooney

performance. When I was a kid, I just thought his scenes were wildly unfunny. Now of course it is obvious to all how offensive those scenes are. It's just one of the million ways we were all asleep back then.

JANUARY 27

It's almost noon. Still waiting to hear about Max. And John and Kate. And Forte. No word from anyone about anything. This journal definitely might turn into a long suicide note.

JANUARY 28

I am very jittery today. I just had a coffee accident in the kitchen, getting wet grounds all over the counter.

Last night, I received a text from Rob at CAA:

I have still not been able to connect with max's agent myself but she told glenn's agent on tues "he seems very into it but we need to speak to him further."

So I hoping to get more info about if they've spoken further and if not what exactly they need to speak further about.

Then this morning I received this from him:

Laura and I are connecting with max and glenn's agent today. From max's agent this am:

I think we are looking good on Max! Let's discuss a plan

So things are almost moving forward. I don't know what to do with myself today so I am going to treat the whole day as a moving meditation. I am going to do the laundry now and wash my car, then later go to Montecito to walk around before I pick up Eve at her boarding school. She's coming home to go to a volleyball tournament in Orange County this weekend.

I just had a second coffee accident, this time getting wet grounds all over the floor. Jittery.

On the way to school this morning, I noticed a car with the license plate HOT2TRT. I pulled up alongside the car and looked inside. A man in his seventies or eighties was driving. He had tons of white hair all over his head and face. He didn't look at all hot to trot.

"Do you think he looks hot to trot?" I asked Henry. Henry gave him a look.

"No," he said.

There was a woman in the passenger seat about his age. "Do you think she is hot to trot?" I asked.

"No," he said.

"Well, maybe he once was," I said.

"He wasn't," Henry said. "And neither was she. You can tell when old people used to be good-looking."

"Hmm," I said, not sure that is always the case.

"Like Grandma," he said. "You can tell she used to be good-looking."

"You should say that to her," I said. He was silent for a moment.

"This might be a weird question," he said.

"Can't wait," I said.

"Has Grandma not had sex for a long time?"

"Not since Grandpa died," I said, although of course now that I think about it, and even though it seems highly unlikely, I can't know that for sure.

Something about the way he asked made me feel Henry felt sad for her.

"She's eighty-six," I said. "I don't think she cares. Things slow down a lot when you're her age."

It's been a full week since I met with John and Kate.

"I think I'm being rejected for—" I just told my Kate, naming the other writer they were going to meet with.

"It's a real low point," she said.

JANUARY 29

It doesn't seem as if Laura and Rob connected with Glenn and Max's agents yesterday, since I never heard about it.

When I was little, I was scared of fun house mirrors. I don't remember actually being in a fun house and seeing myself in a fun house mirror as much as I remember seeing them in TV shows and movies, such as *The Lady from Shanghai* or *The Hardy Boys/Nancy Drew Mysteries*. There was something deeply disturbing about a usually good-looking person looking in a mirror and seeing a hideous grotesque version of him or herself.

For some reason, the idea of that happening filled me with intense fear.

Now when I drive around Los Angeles, much of the time I feel like I am looking at the fun house mirror version of Los Angeles, and again, I am filled with intense fear.

JANUARY 30

Sometimes I wake up and I am so happy not to be in my dreams.

JANUARY 31

It's late Monday morning. Kate Berlant and John Early emailed that they've decided to go with me. We are having a lunch later this week to talk more. I am not sure how I feel. In this moment, everything fills me with dread. I just read in the newspaper about how New Hampshire is trying to get teachers reported for teaching anything "negative" about this country to their students. How can this be happening?

I think about Obama's "two steps forward, one step backward" view on progress. It feels right now like we are taking three steps backward with no end in sight.

Still haven't heard from Rob and Laura about Glenn and Max.

I am going mad today from the state of the world and the state of my waiting for things to happen professionally. Therefore, I am now going to make white bean dip, which takes a while, then chickpea fake tuna salad to have for lunch, then black bean burgers, which really take a while to make, to have for dinner later. And that is how I am going to get through my day.

12:55 P.M.

I am taking a break from all the beans because I just read that Howard Hesseman died over the weekend, which made me think about *WKRP in Cincinnati*. It was never one of my favorite shows as a kid, but I did enjoy it, the first few seasons especially. It rarely made me laugh, but the ensemble cast was so good and subtly soulful. It was a pleasant place to be, similar to *Barney Miller*, although that, of course, was much, much funnier. The actors in both casts had a certain poignance, and the main characters all seemed to be lonely in a way, except that they had each other. Kate had a teacher at NYU who said all TV shows are about families, and maybe he is right.

Then I started thinking about Loni Anderson. I always thought she was a little strange looking. I then remembered something that happened one day, many years ago, when I was an assistant to a television producer. We were at Hamburger Hamlet on Sunset and Doheny, where we met for lunch each day. Some days, that was all we did because he was between jobs.

Somehow we got on the topic of Loni Anderson, and I told him I found her looks a little odd.

"Well, no one else thinks that," he said.

"I'm sure some people do," I said.

"No," he said. "She is considered a great beauty."

"A great beauty?" I said in disbelief.

"Yes," he said.

"No," I said. "Mia Farrow is a great beauty, not Loni Anderson." I don't know why Mia Farrow was the first name that came to me, but it was.

"The world disagrees with you," he said. "The world thinks Loni Anderson is much prettier than Mia Farrow."

"They really don't," I said.

"Fine," he said. "Let's ask the world." He turned to the strangers at the next table.

"Excuse me," he said. "We have a question for you."

I can't remember what they said, or how many people were at the table, but they were open to hearing a question. And he asked them.

"Loni Anderson," they all said.

"See?" he said to me.

After they went back to eating, I said, "That's just them."

"No," he said. "It's everyone."

He then proceeded to ask all the people at the nearby tables. "Loni Anderson," they all said.

"Okay," I finally said to him. "You're right."

I was so sure I was right, and then I wasn't. Which happens a lot to me. Especially about what I think the world wants or thinks.

FEBRUARY 1

The love theme from *The Accidental Tourist* came on the radio yesterday. It was so beautiful and sweet and made me think fondly of the movie. I usually retain which movie theater I saw a movie in, but this time I am drawing a blank. I think it was in Westwood. When it came out, Westwood was swarming with young people on Friday and Saturday nights, and cars would move very, very slowly through the crowded streets. Then for some reason that stopped.

It's strange now to think about how a small story like *The Accidental Tourist* was made into a studio film with movie stars and that is what you would see in an enormous old theater on a Saturday night back then. Also, that there would be several of those released on the same day. It all feels like a different world.

It's like I used to live in one world and now I live in another world. I don't remember my parents feeling this way, but maybe they did. On the other hand, maybe they didn't. It is thirty-four years after *The Accidental Tourist*, and nothing seems the same, especially during this pandemic time. But thirty years prior to *The Accidental Tourist* was 1958. That world had similar movies to go to on a Saturday night. My world is very different from when I was in my twenties in a way that my parents' world wasn't.

It's nine in the morning and I have already swept the kitchen floor twice. I did it once when I woke up and just did it again because I noticed there were still tons of crumbs and dust everywhere. It's like the broom I bought a few weeks ago is refusing to do its job.

Still no word on Max Barbakow, and no talk of what the next steps are for the Glenn Close project. Nothing from Evan, who was supposed to set up a Zoom with Will Forte for the New Zealand idea. And waiting for a lunch confirmation from John and Kate.

FEBRUARY 2

I kept constantly checking my email all day yesterday, waiting to hear something about anything. Finally around four in the afternoon, two emails came in. First, John and Kate confirmed lunch for Friday, then over the next fourteen hours, it moved to Thursday, and now it is to be on Saturday. The other came from Laura, announcing that my Glenn Close project is moving forward with Max attached. The script is scheduled to be sent to networks/streamers next week. I was so agitated by all the waiting that oddly, even after hearing something, I am still today in an agitated state.

Everything has become so slow and can be undone at any moment that moving forward doesn't even feel like moving forward.

The air handler situation hasn't moved forward at all. I am waiting for Damon, our former contractor, to send someone to remove the adjacent wall panel so the old air handler can be taken out without causing damage to the walls. Damon was supposed to come days ago but canceled and hasn't rescheduled. I just texted him for an update. I texted:

Damon, it's cold.

An hour has gone by, and still no response from Damon.

All day yesterday, I was waiting for an update on Glenn and Max, now I am waiting for an update from Damon. Life is what happens when you are waiting for an update.

Once, many, many years ago, I was waiting and waiting in the reception area of Comedy Central in New York City. My agent had scheduled some meeting that I didn't want to go to.

"Come on," I said when she originally told me about the meeting.

"What do you mean?" she said.

"Eh," I said. "It's Comedy Central."

But I agreed to have the meeting. Then I got there a few minutes before the meeting. And just sat in the reception area for almost an hour.

I was getting more and more upset until finally I called my agent and told her how long I had been waiting there.

"Can I leave?" I said.

"No," she said. "Just give them a few more minutes." Finally I did have a meeting with whoever the person was. They made some bad excuse for their lateness, and I of course said it wasn't a problem, even though it was.

I could never have known then that one day my life, day in and day out, would feel like that hour at Comedy Central where I just waited.

One other thing—when I was at the gym earlier today, by accident, I stole a man's phone, and now he hates me.

I was getting dressed, about to leave the gym, when a distraught man came up to me and said angrily, "You have my phone."

I looked in my bag, and there his phone was, underneath my phone. I have no idea how I grabbed it and then didn't realize it. I had taken a quick shower, so I could only have stolen it for less than ten minutes, but he was still very mad at me.

"I'm sorry," I said. "I don't know how it happened." He grunted at me with hatred, turned around, and walked away.

FEBRUARY 3

At the gym today, I was on a bicycle when suddenly the man who hates me got on the next machine, which is some kind of elliptical thing where you go up and down very fast. I wanted to apologize again, but felt he didn't want that. I thought about making a move for his phone as a joke but then thought better of it. It felt odd to be so close to him. I wanted to get up and go do something else, but felt that would be odd too. So I just stayed there, outlasting him, very uncomfortable the whole time.

Damon's men came to remove the wall panel, so we are slowly moving forward to getting heat in that part of the house. I just called the air handler people, and they are scheduled to come for the third time on Monday.

FEBRUARY 4

Everything here is broken. Among other things, there were several leaks during the last big rain. I called the roofers and haven't heard back. Also, I need new tires and can't bring myself to bring the car into the car place to get them because the car place depresses me.

And Just Like That . . . depresses me. It ended last night, so I have had to read about it everywhere. Everyone in the world has to write about it, for some unknown reason. I stopped watching it because it wasn't fun for me. The main characters don't seem as smart as they used to be, and sometimes when I watch dim people on television their voices start to feel like they are inside my brain, making me stupider.

That's how I felt watching *And Just Like That . . .* , which feels like today's world, while *Sex and the City*, a show I loved and will always love and still watch when I am on an airplane, feels like the previous world.

Maybe part of the reason I can't enjoy *And Just Like That . . .* is it also reminds me that my old friend Willie, who played Stanford Blatch, is not here. It has been months since he died, and it still seems impossible to believe. Part of me still pretends that he isn't gone and I just haven't seen him lately, and watching *And Just Like That . . .* makes it harder for me to pretend that.

I'm struggling with the waiting today. It is nice that Max Barbakow is finally attached to the Glenn Close script and it is going out into the world. But for some reason, it is not going to go out until next week, even though today is Friday. So it feels like this will take at least a month to play out. And there is no reason to believe anyone will even want to buy it.

I have John and Kate for lunch tomorrow, so I should be watching some of their material, but for some reason I feel resistant. I guess it feels like it is just more work that I am doing without getting paid. I have been doing so much of that for the last year, trying to get my ideas for a television show off the ground.

I'm curious to see if someone buys the John and Kate project. When I had my deal at Sony, anything that I thought would be interesting to supervise turned out to not be what the world wanted. I never sold one project during my two-year deal at Sony. I had ideas no one bought, and then, when they would come to me to supervise things, none of the ones I picked to go out with sold either.

So not only does the world not seem to want what I want to write, but it also seems not to want what I would like to see.

I heard "Take My Breath Away" on the radio as I was driving earlier. I never saw *Top Gun*, so it doesn't remind me of it, but it does remind me of the music video, which had scenes from *Top Gun* in it. And it reminds me of who I was at that time. When that song was on the radio every five seconds, I was really in the old world, not this world. And I was so young, I mean really young. It felt like there was so much out there, just waiting to take my breath away.

I came home from Vicente Foods Market today and, as I unpacked my bag, realized I hadn't gotten butter, the one thing I had gone there for. I got back in the car and went back and got the butter. Sadly, that is the second time this week I went to Vicente Foods and didn't get the one thing I went there for. I blame the waiting.

Two things that picked me up this afternoon:

I heard the most haunting song on the radio called "One Afternoon" by the Bob James Trio. I listen to the classical music station all the time, and they play the same things over and over, yet I never heard this one before. I can't believe how much it touched me.

Then, at the end of the day, I jumped rope and turned on TCM to soothe myself. I caught the last fifteen minutes of *Key Largo*, which was not one of my favorite Humphrey Bogart movies when I was a kid. But as an adult I have come to love it, especially the last fifteen minutes, which always seem to be on when I turn on TCM. Again, like "One Afternoon," I was stunned by its beauty and was moved, especially by the final moments when Lauren Bacall gets the phone call that Humphrey Bogart is alive and then opens the blinds, letting in the light.

FEBRUARY 5

Kate Berlant woke up not feeling great, so she emailed to cancel lunch today in case she has COVID. So this lunch, which was supposed to be Friday, then Thursday, then Saturday, is now no day. I told my friend Gary. He texted back:

That's it

I would tell them you're not interested

I answered:

I can't

But I am definitely agitated at the overall lack of forward movement.

FEBRUARY 6

I woke up this morning and for some reason found myself thinking about a woman I worked with in my first job right out of college. Her name was Anna-Mae, and I can't remember what her exact job was. I was a production assistant on a television movie, then graduated to just being an assistant in the office of the three producers of the television movie. I worked for the youngest producer, a former accountant who was in his forties. And Anna-Mae worked on the floor above for the oldest producer, who was ancient. Maybe she was his assistant or maybe she was one of two assistants he had. He had been very successful during the golden age of television, making various very serious dramas about social issues. Anna-Mae seemed old to me too, although not as old as him. She was very buoyant, always in a good mood, never bothered by how crabby her producer always seemed to be.

She would pass through our office with some chicken soup for him, stopping to grab silverware and a napkin.

Once my producer was there as she passed through, and he said to me, "Do you know who Anna-Mae was married to?"

"Oh, come on," she said. "Don't."

"Who?" I said.

"Joseph Kramm," he said. And then looked at me, as if that should mean something.

"Who's that?" I asked.

"I'm going upstairs," Anna-Mae said. But she still fussed around the kitchen area.

"He wrote *The Shrike*," he said.

"Ohhhhhh," I said. *The Shrike* was a movie I would sometimes see on television as a kid. It was based on a play about a man who has a nervous breakdown and is committed to a mental hospital. He has a loving wife who visits him every day, but (I think, but I am not sure) it is slowly revealed that she is the reason for his breakdown. She is a shrike, which means she is a monster who criticizes and undermines him at all times. I think in the end he has to go home with her, even though he has by now fallen in love with someone nicer, and much more normal than the shrike.

I never liked the movie that much, but I think my parents talked about shrikes sometimes, so I was very aware of what a shrike was and how scary and malevolent a shrike could be.

Basically, a shrike was someone you would never want to turn into.

I looked at Anna-Mae.

"So . . . you were the shrike?" I said in disbelief. She seemed like the kindest person in the world.

"No," she said.

"Yes, she was," the producer teased.

"It was all made up," she said. "He was a terrible man."

The producer looked at me and said, "She was the shrike."

"It was fiction," she said. "He was a very disturbed person."

"I can't believe you were the shrike," I said.

"Oh, please," she said to both of us. And then she went upstairs. The play was from the 1950s, so it had all been decades ago, and I think Anna-Mae had later remarried and had a family now.

From then on, whenever we would have a nice moment together, afterward, Anna-Mae would say, "See? Am I a shrike?"

"Not at all," I would say.

I just now looked up the play and Joseph Kramm on the internet, and there is no evidence of his marriage to Anna-Mae, unless she changed her name. I learned that *The Shrike* won the Pulitzer the year it was on Broadway, and that Joseph Kramm never had any real success after that, and died years later while living in a furnished room. The size of the *New York Times* obituary was very small. And, of course, *The Shrike* is never revived, the movie isn't even on TCM, and no one today except me even knows what a shrike is.

When I was young, I thought if you won a Pulitzer, that meant you were guaranteed a glittering, successful life permanently and you would be remembered forever. In fact, I am embarrassed to say part of me still thinks that, even though I just typed the previous paragraph.

Also, there was another dead bird in front of the house this morning.

FEBRUARY 7

It's 8:40 a.m. and I am waiting for the air handler people, who were supposed to be here at 8:00 a.m.

The Glenn Close script is supposed to go out this week. I have no idea if that means it goes out today, or tomorrow, or another day, or if it goes out Friday for a weekend read. I should ask I guess. Here is who they said is getting it:

* Amazon: Ryan Andolina
* Apple: Matt Cherniss, Dana Tuinier
* Netflix: Tracey Pakosta
* Peacock: Jeff Meyerson
* HBO: Amy Gravitt
* HBO Max: Suzanna Makkos, Billy Wee
* Hulu: Billy Rosenberg
* FX: Nick Grad, Kate Lambert
* Paramount+: Nicole Clemens
* Showtime: Amy Israel, Brendan Countee
* Starz: Kathy Busby

It doesn't seem like a Showtime, FX, or HBO show to me. It is a little too upbeat and feel-good. Those places traditionally tend to want something a little harsher. I am hoping HBO Max goes for it, but am worried it is a little "soft" for them too. Everyone says they want a *Ted Lasso*, which the love interest for Glenn has a lot in common with, based on what I've heard of *Ted Lasso* and the five minutes I watched. So maybe that will help it get bought.

Years and years ago, I had a quasi-date with one of the executives on the list. I am pretty sure the quasi-date ruins any hope for this idea being bought by her network. But since I have never seen any show on her network, I am assuming it wouldn't be a good fit for them anyway.

Now it's 9:10 a.m. The air handler people just arrived, thank God. And Kate Berlant emailed that she got a positive on her COVID test this morning. I suggested we have a phone call or Zoom this week to keep things moving.

It feels like I will never hear from Evan Moore about Will Forte for my New Zealand project.

Kate and I were at our friend Nicole's house yesterday. She said her son Joe was punched in the face by a stranger on the Venice boardwalk and her friend Alison got a concussion from being thrown against a wall by a stranger while waiting for an elevator. Kate immediately started talking about what country we should move to.

4:22 P.M.

The air handler people just left. There is still more work to do. Someone is coming between noon and one tomorrow. In more upbeat news, no dead bird today.

5:08 P.M.

The washing machine just mysteriously stopped, even though it wasn't done with its cycle. Two enormous thick towels were in there, and now that they haven't gone through a spin cycle, they are now the two heaviest towels in the world.

Before putting them in the dryer, I squatted on the bathroom floor and squeezed water out of them into the shower. So it seems that something must be wrong with the washing machine.

Last week, my brother Andrew texted "Get out of here, Finchley" to me and my other brother Michael. It was a reference to a *Twilight Zone* where all the appliances in a house turn against the owner, and they yell "Get out of here, Finchley" to him. I've become Finchley.

FEBRUARY 8

I went to Vicente Foods after dropping Henry off at school and came home without the thing I wanted to get, so it's a two-trip-to–Vicente Foods day.

The air handler people have somehow turned off the heat in the part of the house with the working air handler, so when the person comes at noon, they will hopefully fix that. But at this moment, the air handler people have officially taken us backward.

I just checked in with Laura at CAA to ask when exactly the Glenn script is going out to people. She said they are waiting, because Max wanted to talk to his agent one more time before the script went out. She doesn't know why. I now have a weight on my chest.

I am supposed to have a phone call with John and Kate Thursday. And of course no word from Evan about Will Forte.

12:00 P.M.

Two new men arrived from the heating place. They have no idea why they are here or what they are supposed to do. I am not sure how to handle this.

12:34 PM

There have been a lot of phone calls to Lena, the woman who answers the phone at the heater repair place. Lena wants to know what the two men are supposed to do.

"They're supposed to fix the one that was working up until yesterday when the two men did something as they looked at it to figure out how to install the new one," I said. "And then there was one last step to installing the new one that the two men yesterday said someone would finish today. My wife says it has something to do with a liquid."

"I'm not a heating person," I said at one point. "So I don't know what is happening."

At this moment, the men have figured out why the heating unit that didn't need repairs wasn't working—the men who came yesterday turned it off when they looked at it to see how to install the one that doesn't work.

It has been ascertained that the new one needs refrigerant, and now they have left to go get refrigerant and bring it back and put it in.

I asked Laura to get more information from Max's agent, and she responded that he is committed to the project but feels it is "all moving so quickly" after having had only one conversation. I offered to have another conversation with him. I'm going to jump rope now because I don't know what else to do.

4:44 P.M.

Just came back from trip number two to Vicente Foods. The new air handler is installed and working. Now all we need is Damon's men to come back and put the wall panels back in. No word from Laura about Max.

FEBRUARY 9

Sometimes I think about a moment that happened almost ten years ago. I was in New York for work for a week or so, and I flew back on a Friday morning and arrived in time to pick up Henry and Eve after school. I parked in the lot at school and got out of the car and walked around the campus, looking for them. I spotted Eve a hundred feet away playing with her friends. She then looked up, saw me, and immediately broke into the fastest run toward me, as if she couldn't get to me quick enough. It was the most moving thing that ever happened to me. Never again has she been so glad to see me, but having it happen once was enough.

It's starting to feel as if this Glenn Close script is not going out this week. I will email Evan, the producer on the New Zealand idea, to ask what happened to Will Forte.

Okay, here is what I wrote:

Hello, hope all is well. Any news re: Will?

4:09 P.M.

Still no news on Max. Evan did respond about Will Forte though. Here is what he wrote:

Hey Bruce!

I texted him today and will give him a ring if he doesn't get back to me. In the meantime, thought it would be helpful to craft a small list of filmmakers (or other actors) that could be meaningful and/or have ties to NZ (or both, ideally). Let me know if anyone comes to mind on your end, I'll put some names together.

Hmmm. This doesn't seem promising at all to me. He can put some names together, but I really don't have any desire to.

FEBRUARY 10

It is an unusually hot day, and the sunlight seems even more beautiful than normal. It makes the green bamboo I can see outside the window almost yellow. I wonder if it would be possible for me to spend an entire day fully content to enjoy the sunlight, not thinking about anything else. I would like to try.

When I was in elementary school, there was a game (although I am not sure it is correct usage of the word to call it a game) where you would say to another kid, "Say hi to your knee."

"Why?" the other kid would say. "Just do it," you would say. "Okay, hi knee!" the other kid would reluctantly say.

Then you would laugh and say, "I made you say heinie," which was a slang word for your butt.

And that was the whole game. Maybe it's more of a trick than a game. Now that I am thinking about it, I remember I had a teacher who used to tell us to sit on our heinies. I never hear anyone say "heinie" anymore.

No word from Laura about Max. I can't bear to ask her for an update, so I am not going to. I feel like I am being tortured.

This is much, much worse than being tricked into saying "heinie."

2:00 P.M.

Just had a two-hour meeting with John and Kate Berlant to discuss their idea. I really like them and enjoy the things they think about.

During the meeting I got an email from Laura. She says that Max wants us all to have another meeting to talk about where the script is going, before it actually goes out. So as today is Thursday, it is definitely not going out to people this week.

Damon's men are here now putting the wall panels up, so hopefully when they leave, this air handler chapter of my life will be over.

2:23 P.M.

There is a problem putting the panels back in. There is a big space between them that wasn't there before. They are the same exact panels that used to have no space between them, so it defies any rational explanation how there is now a space.

2:41 P.M.

Everyone gave up. The panels will now have a space between them. I'm choosing to look at this as a way to have more space in my life. Maybe every situation is an opportunity for acceptance. I'm not sure what else to think.

FEBRUARY 11

I just came back from Vicente Foods. I almost left without getting the one thing I went there for, but I remembered right as I reached the register, so only one trip today! It was a true triumph.

One of the most triumphant moments of my life happened at LEGOLAND, a place I love, even though I hate most amusement parks, especially Disneyland. Disneyland sickens me.

I love LEGOLAND because of its low-key charm and sweet little rides and weird little shows. It's an amusement park with heart. I could go there right now by myself and have a good time wandering around. The day of my triumph was years ago when the kids were little and were both *Despicable Me* fans. There was an area that had stalls that had various games, like there are at the Santa Monica pier. There was one of those games where you get three tries at throwing a beanbag or something at a target, and if you get it close enough to the middle all three times, you got a big stuffed bright yellow Minion from *Despicable Me*.

Henry and Eve both really wanted a big Minion and they tried several times, but neither was able to win one. Toward the end of the day, after going on all the rides they wanted to, Eve said, "Let's go back to get a Minion."

"Are you sure?" I said. It seemed like it would just be more losses for them.

"Yes," she said. Henry was also adamant about trying again.

We went to the area with the games. The man at the Minion place nodded at me as we arrived, as if to say, "You guys again."

Eve made Henry go first. He got one beanbag in the center and then another beanbag in the center.

"This is crazy," I said to Kate. He hadn't done nearly as well on the other earlier tries.

"I know," she said. I was now extremely nervous. I wouldn't be able to bear the inevitable.

Henry threw the third one, and it went in the center. We all whooped and Henry got a big Minion.

There is a feeling for me when Henry wins something that is unlike any other. Henry winning something is the greatest feeling of all.

Now Eve was up. She threw a beanbag, and it went in the center. She threw her second one, and it went in the center.

This is nuts, I thought, although truthfully she had better aim usually than Henry, so it wasn't as surprising.

Eve turned to me.

"You do it," she said. Shit, I thought. But it was so unusual for her to ask me for something like this that I knew I had to rise to the moment.

I took the beanbag and threw it. It hit the center. We whooped again, and Eve got her big Minion.

As I said, it is one of my most triumphant moments. In fact, I can't think of that many other ones.

It is now years and years later, both Henry and Eve have gotten rid of most of their stuffed animals, but the Minions still live with us. I'm never letting anyone get rid of those Minions.

Oh, Laura's assistant emailed. Max Barbakow has some dates and times he can meet with me and Glenn next Tuesday, Wednesday, Thursday, or Friday. She wanted to see which ones I can do before asking Glenn.

I can do any of them, I wrote back. It now seems unlikely that the script will be able to go out to buyers next week. I am starting to have a grudge against Max. A big grudge.

But I want to go back to amusement parks. My father had a mysterious amusement park story he used to tell that seems like it can't be true. When he was a teenager, he and a friend of his both liked the same girl. The three of them went to an amusement park one night. At one point in the evening, they went on a Ferris wheel, where the three of them sat together, with the girl in the middle. After the wheel went round and round, up and down, a few times, my father looked at the girl, and her face was turning a weird color and she had an odd expression as she stared at him.

She's going to throw up, he thought. So he instinctively put his hand to her face and pushed it so she was looking at his friend. And the girl threw up on the friend.

The whole pushing-her-face move seems extremely out of character for my father. Even the fact that he told the story seems very out of character for him.

Can it possibly be true? He is dead and there is no one I can ask, so I will never know, which is sad to me.

I just saw that in the backyard there is an enormous amount of unfamiliar animal excrement. It is right in the center of the backyard, and I have to go clean it up, because if I don't there is absolutely no scenario that Henry wouldn't step in it.

FEBRUARY 12

It's Saturday. I got an email from Laura's assistant at the end of the day that Glenn didn't respond with any days/times. So the meeting with Max still isn't scheduled.

When I told Kate that Max wants to talk about where the show is going, she had a different interpretation than I did of what he wants to talk about. I thought he wants to talk about what places the script is going to, and she thinks he wants to talk about what direction the series is going in, future stories, etc. Maybe she is right. But I should definitely figure out which it is before having the meeting.

Last night, Kate and I tried to finish watching *Ordinary People* on the television in the living room. We stood there for quite some time, struggling to get the television set on, which requires several steps, the last one being a mystery that I can sometimes do and sometimes not do, while Henry can always do it. He was at the school play, so we didn't have him to help. We finally gave up and watched the last third of it on her laptop and had a good cry. It was the best thing I have watched or, to be more exact, rewatched in recent memory.

My personal goal for the day is to learn how to always be able to turn the television on. I am going to get a lesson from Henry this morning because he is at the school play again tonight and we will be on our own with the television again.

A convoy of antivax truckers have been wreaking havoc in Canada for what seems like weeks, and now other countries have antivax truckers having tantrums. Also, I keep reading that Russia is going to invade Ukraine and then World War III will start.

I'm really not in the mood for World War III.

FEBRUARY 13

I was able to turn on the television last night without Henry. However, I didn't feel it was a result of his lesson that morning. I was still fumbling in the dark, guessing, on the last step as always. I just happened to be able to do it, as I often am. It was reminiscent of taking a test and guessing on the answers and doing well, but knowing you don't really know the material.

I was just now doing battle with a lawn hose outside, desperately trying to untangle it. The more I tried to untangle it, the more it got tangled. It was like being in a dream. I often have dreams where I am trying to pick something up, but it just keeps slipping out of my fingers for no discernible reason.

I live in a small house in a metropolitan city, but it often feels like I have an enormous farm out in the country and I am tending to all the various things you need to tend to on a farm, and failing.

FEBRUARY 14

It's a little after noon on Monday. I just heard an ominous sound and went to check to see if a bird flew into the front or back windows. I was very nervous, but luckily I didn't find any casualties in the front or back.

Still no word from Glenn about when we will meet with Max. I find silence from the world on Mondays harder than silence from the world on other days, not that I have that easy a time with the silence in any case.

If Max hadn't asked for the extra meeting, then today would have possibly been a day when I heard if someone was interested in potentially buying the project, and that somehow makes the silence worse.

The feeling reminds me of when I was twenty-two and had broken up with my girlfriend at the time. Even though I was the one who had ended the relationship, I still mourned the death of it. We had gone to Europe during the summer, and during each week of the following summer I would think, oh, this is when we were in Paris, or this is when we were in Venice, or this is when we were in Greece.

Oh, this is when I would have heard if someone wanted to buy this project.

It's Valentine's Day, and since I have nothing better to do, I am planning to make vegan stuffed cabbage rolls. Kate's grandmother made stuffed cabbage rolls and she has fond memories of them from her childhood. I have never eaten a stuffed cabbage roll. I looked at many recipes for vegan ones, and they all seem very daunting. I am extremely nervous.

I don't miss anything my grandmother cooked. She made apple pies that everyone said were delicious, but they tasted terrible to me, especially her crust, which never seemed to cover the whole pie. There were always gaps in the pie where you could see the inside. No one else minded but me.

"Eh," I can hear my grandmother say. "Who needs more crust?"

All normal people do, I would think to myself. The crust should cover the pie, except for the hole on top.

There are so many things I do miss, though, too many to count. Sometimes it seems like I spend my whole day missing things.

I am doing the laundry right now, and it makes me think that one thing I really miss is doing the laundry when Henry and Eve were little. Children's clothes are so small and strange and colorful and sometimes have something bizarre written on them, like "Go for It." I would kill to fold those odd little shirts and pants and dresses today.

FEBRUARY 15

The vegan mushroom tempeh stuffed cabbage rolls were okay, but definitely, definitely not in a rush to make that one again.

While I was stuffing the tempeh and mushrooms into the cabbage leaves, I got an email saying that Glenn had finally picked a time and day to meet. Naturally, it was the last time and day Max offered, which is this Friday at nine in the morning. This has really slowed down to a crawl.

In the car on the way to school today, Henry asked me what I was going to do today.

"I have to look over some notes Kate and John sent me," I said. "I have a meeting with them tomorrow."

"Your days are really empty," he said.

"Yeah," I said.

"Remember how busy you were this time last year?" he said.

"Yeah."

I was on set fifteen hours a day last February. When I think back to being on the set a year ago, almost all I remember is how bad the food was. Usually, when I think back to being on set for a television show, all I remember is if the food was good or bad and if I was too hot or too cold that day.

A few moments later in the car ride, Henry asked me if I ever cared about his waking me up early in the mornings when he was little.

"No," I said. "Why do you ask?"

He explained he had been watching a comedian who complained about how his little kids woke him up when he wanted to sleep later.

"I never minded," I said. "I liked seeing you. Someone waking me up never bothers me. Even when Mom wakes me up in the middle of the night. It just doesn't bother me. A million things bother me, but that's not one of them."

"Like what?" he asked.

"Traffic, obviously," I said, because he has seen me go insane in traffic.

"And politics," he said.

"That's not exactly true," I said. "Red state people don't bother me as much as they frighten me."

12:00 P.M.

I just got an email from John, who is visiting his family in Nashville. Things are too "crazy" for him to meet tomorrow, so we are going to push it until next week sometime.

In a script, every scene should move the story forward. No scenes should be in a script unless there is a reason for them to be there. If my life were a script, I would leave out the last few weeks. Maybe longer.

5:22 P.M.

A couple of hours ago, I was coming out of the bank and I saw an unfamiliar sign for another business a few feet away. It was for an Infrared Sauna Bar. It had a picture of a little pod you could crawl into, and after half an hour all your problems could be solved. I sat staring at the picture of the pod for several minutes, wondering whether this was what I needed to change my life. Then decided it wasn't.

A few minutes later, in the car, I was thinking for some reason about a disagreement I had with one of the other American producers of the TV show I worked on in New Zealand last year.

There were all these billboards on the highway outside Wellington that had a picture of a scared person in a car. And the sign read Slow Down with a handwritten "Me" between the Slow and the Down.

"Why does it say 'me'?" Kate asked once. "It's not me."

"I stare at it all the time and have no idea what it means," I said. "Whatever it is, it doesn't really make sense."

This was true of a lot of things in New Zealand.

"I don't even think drivers in New Zealand are that aggressive," I said.

Later, when I was talking about the sign with the producer, he said, "The drivers here are very aggressive."

"It's a lot worse in Los Angeles," I said. "The drivers there are much scarier."

"No, they aren't," he said adamantly.

"Yes, they definitely are," I insisted. Both of us had lived in Los Angeles and were now both living in Wellington, but each of us was firm in our differing beliefs about our experiences.

It's a real reminder. Everything that happens to us only happens to us.

FEBRUARY 16

Nothing to do workwise today, so I tried to just be and was fairly successful.

When I try to just be, I think of this Buddhist quote: Before enlightenment, chop wood, carry water. After enlightenment, chop wood, carry water.

As I understand it, the quote means you can be content doing your daily tasks if you are fully present while doing them. You just chop wood or carry water and be in the moment, not thinking of other things.

The highlight of my chop-wood-carry-water day came unexpectedly while making vegan mayonnaise in the kitchen. I had put on an hour of Henry Mancini music from YouTube, but then I started to notice the music wasn't composed by Mancini but was, I believe, music played by his orchestra.

So as I was listening to various non-Mancini songs like

"Stardust" and "The Way We Were," suddenly a song came on that I hadn't heard in decades. It was "Nadia's Theme" and it was one of the best few minutes ever.

"Nadia's Theme" is actually music from *The Young and the Restless*, but it is called "Nadia's Theme" because when I was a kid there was a gymnast named Nadia Comăneci who was in the Olympics and used the music for one of her routines. She was amazing to watch, almost poetic. And her artistry made this music, which perhaps could be thought of as something that was not much, become something almost magical. Nadia turned the music under the opening credits of a soap opera into art.

From then on, "Nadia's Theme" was everywhere, maybe even playing on the top forty stations, which I still listen to today, even though they are not called top forty stations anymore.

It turns out that the man who composed the music was Barry De Vorzon. I knew the name when I was a kid because my brother Andrew was friends with a kid named Mark Dwartzan, and Barry was his uncle.

The fact that he changed his name from Dwartzan to De Vorzon captured our imaginations. With just a few letters you could elevate yourself. Instead of having a shlumpy name and existence, you could have something more inspired and magical. And, of course, the magic was compounded when his music for a soap opera became art through Nadia and her routine.

I feel as if I had somehow forgotten about "Nadia's Theme" and now I never will again. I just played it again as I wrote this.

FEBRUARY 17

I went to a party when I was in my twenties, probably about three decades ago. There was a psychic at the party. I waited for a long time to have a reading with her, but finally it was my turn. I only remember one thing she said to me.

"Someday you're going to win an Academy Award," she said.

"I am?" I said, surprised. I was trying to be a television writer mostly, not very focused on writing movies.

"Yes," she said. Then her expression changed a bit. "But it's going to be a *reallllly* long time before that happens."

I think we can now officially say it's been a really long time. With no end in sight.

I have to prepare today for my meeting with Glenn and Max. I still don't know what to prepare and am resentful about having to have this meeting. This resentment is making me not have any ideas.

I am going to put on music from YouTube that is supposed to clear negative energy and bounce on the mini-trampoline for twenty minutes and hope that helps me.

TWENTY MINUTES LATER

You know what? It actually worked. I have some ideas of what to say tomorrow. I highly recommend the YouTube clearing-negative-energy music

FEBRUARY 18

I had my meeting with Glenn and Max at nine this morning. Glenn didn't show up until about forty minutes in, but I had a nice time talking to Max. I think he's smart and he has a good heart and I like how he talks about the script and characters. So after Glenn showed up, we talked for another twenty minutes, and everyone agreed that they are comfortable with the script going out to buyers next week.

Oh, Kate, of course, was right. Max did want to talk more about where the show and characters were going, and he had a few questions about what our pitch would be if anyone wanted to meet after reading the script. I said it would be informal, less of a pitch and more of a conversation. I would talk about my goals for the show, and ideally he and Glenn would talk about what they connected with in the show.

When the meeting ended at ten, I was exhausted. It was like I was ready for bed. I guess I was nervous about the meeting, as at this point it feels like this is all I have that the world might possibly want, so if it goes wrong at any point, then I don't know where else I will turn for work.

Kate is with Eve in Las Vegas for a volleyball tournament, so it is just Henry and me. Tonight we are going to have pizza for dinner then watch *The Twilight Zone* episode where the machines turn against Finchley. It is my idea of a perfect evening.

The Twilight Zone is such a singular television show, in my opinion. I mean, of course, there is nothing else like it. But more than that, when I watch some episodes, I feel like I am watching art, which is almost never how I feel watching a television show. At best, I can be moved or delighted or be interested. But in some of the best episodes of *The Twilight Zone* I feel touched in a way that only art can touch me. If *The Twilight Zone* didn't exist, the world would be such a worse place.

When I was a kid, I was gripped by the *Twilight Zone* episode where Vera Miles is waiting for a bus in an empty bus station at night and sees another Vera Miles in the same bus station. That is all I will say, but it got inside me and haunted me and still does. And there was just so much emotional weight and fear and sadness in the episode.

FEBRUARY 19

I had a going-to-Staples-to-get-something/Staples-not-having-it/ going-to-another-Staples day. This happened multiple times in multiple ways. I drove all the way to Culver City to get my favorite turkey sandwich, and, oddly, the restaurant was out of turkey.

I have not always had, but have had for a long time, the dream of having a book published with a cover that is just the title and my name, no art of any kind. For me, that would mean I really had become someone.

Some days I wish I didn't want to be someone. Most days.

I've been cleaning, and from the corner of my eye, I thought I just spied an animal in the living room, but it was my vacuum.

FEBRUARY 20

I heard a bird outside today and it made me miss the birds of New Zealand. They are much higher pitched, which makes them feel much more emotional than American birds, and they make urgent sounds that are impossible to ignore. It's like they're really trying to tell you something, although, of course, you never know what. I feel like them today.

It's Sunday. Here is my week ahead. Tomorrow is Presidents' Day. Some men come at nine to service the water heater. We have the most delicate water heater, which needs tending to every few months. It's "green," of course, which makes it much more delicate than a machine has any right to be. Then Tuesday I fly to New York. Wednesday, I have a Zoom meeting with John and Kate. And, of course, supposedly the Glenn Close script goes out to buyers by Friday.

I just jumped rope while watching Oprah talk to Reverend Michael Beckwith on her *Super Soul Sunday* TV show. I am now determined to have a higher vibration, thanks to Michael's inspiring words.

10:45 A.M.

The first few lines of "Pure Imagination" just popped into my head. It's the song Gene Wilder sings in *Willy Wonka & the Chocolate*

Factory. Later in the song he sings, "Want to change the world? There's nothing to it." In this moment, that actually feels true to me. And I definitely do want to change the world.

"If you want to view paradise, simply look around and view it," he sings. I mean, this song has all the answers.

I remember seeing *Willy Wonka & the Chocolate Factory* at the Maplewood movie theater. I was only six when it came out. Maybe I saw it with my older brothers, but in my memory, when the movie ended and the lights came up, I floated out of the theater and I walked home alone, totally at peace with the world. "Pure Imagination" was in my head and I felt like anything was possible, and I am still that person today even when I don't seem like it.

3:45 P.M.

Henry is out having his first driving lesson. I am not sure how I am supposed to do anything other than wait for him to come home alive.

6:12 P.M.

He's alive. I decided to try to use up what's in the refrigerator before we leave on Tuesday, so I made a vegan broccoli soup that actually turned out good by some miracle. In some way, I feel Reverend Michael Beckwith is responsible. He's changed my whole life. Here is the recipe from a website called Love & Lemons, but I substituted a can of chickpeas for a potato.

VEGAN BROCCOLI SOUP

INGREDIENTS
- 2 tablespoons extra-virgin olive oil, more for drizzling
- 1 small yellow onion, diced
- 1/2 cup chopped celery

- 1/2 cup chopped carrots
- 1 pound broccoli, stems diced, florets chopped
- 1 small Yukon Gold potato, diced (1 cup)
- 4 garlic cloves, minced
- 4 cups vegetable broth
- 3 cups cubed bread, for croutons
- 1/2 cup raw cashews
- 1 1/2 teaspoons apple cider vinegar
- 1/2 teaspoon Dijon mustard
- 1/3 cup fresh dill
- 1 tablespoon fresh lemon juice
- 3/4 teaspoon sea salt
- Freshly ground black pepper

DIRECTIONS

Preheat the oven to 350°F and line two small baking sheets
with parchment paper.

Heat the oil in a large pot or Dutch oven over medium
heat. Add the onion, celery, carrots, broccoli stems (put the
florets aside), salt, and pepper and sauté until softened, about
10 minutes.

Add the potatoes and garlic and stir, then add the broth
and simmer for 20 minutes until the potatoes are soft. Let
cool slightly.

Set aside 1 cup of the broccoli florets to roast as a topping
for the soup. Place the remaining florets in a steamer basket
and set over a pot with one inch of water. Bring the water to
a simmer, cover, and let steam 5 minutes, until the broccoli is
tender.

Meanwhile, place the reserved broccoli florets and the bread
cubes on the baking sheets. Toss with a drizzle of olive oil and a

pinch of salt. Roast until the bread is crispy and the broccoli is tender and browned around the edges, 10 to 15 minutes.

Transfer the soup to the blender and add the cashews, apple cider vinegar, and mustard, and blend until creamy. Work in batches, if necessary.

Add the steamed broccoli florets, dill, and lemon juice, and pulse until the broccoli is incorporated but still chunky. The soup should be thick; if it's too thick, add 1/2 cup water to thin to your desired consistency.

Season to taste and serve the soup in bowls with the roasted broccoli and croutons on top.

We already had homemade croutons, so didn't need to make them, thank God. And I didn't roast any broccoli. And didn't have celery. And added a lot of brewer's yeast and turmeric, which I now add to everything. I'm telling you, this soup really turned out good.

There is an owl outside, singing, "Hoo hoo, hoo! Hoo hoo, hoo!" and all feels right with the world.

FEBRUARY 21

The man who is now working on the water heater has a MAGA feeling about him, but I am trying to spread love, not fear, in our interactions.

11:07 A.M.

There is some problem with something and the man has to leave to get a gasket and come back between three and five to put the gasket in. I have no idea what a gasket is.

11:15 A.M.

Now he says he is not coming back today. He is going to come back with the gasket when Henry and I come back from New York. So it will hopefully be next week sometime. It's now become an ongoing air handler type of situation.

Is there any way my life could be turned into a musical about nothing ever happening and nothing ever getting fixed?

6:03 P.M.

I lost my ticket in a parking structure and had to pay the maximum. Technically, I didn't lose it. I watched the ticket float down into a space between two parts of the back of my car where there is a space because I slammed my car into a pillar in the same parking structure months ago.

I often slam my car into parking structure pillars. Am I the only one? I once saw my friend Winnie do it right after we had dinner and we both collapsed into total hysterical laughter.

So I'm not the only one. But are Winnie and I the only ones who do it?

I paid the full price, and tried to put it behind me. And yet. It makes me wonder, Isn't there something heartless about making you pay the maximum if you lose your ticket? I wish we lived in a world where parking structures were kinder and more charitable to people who make mistakes.

FEBRUARY 22

I am on an early-morning flight to New York with Henry, hoping there will be no maskless screaming person harassing a flight attendant and getting violent.

I am trying to be less tense, so I am listening to one of the audio mixes the flight offers. It is labeled Chill but so far it isn't working.

A FEW MINUTES LATER
Actually, the Chill music really worked.

5:30 P.M.
Ellyn is texting me to say that she emailed Rob and Laura to hear if Glenn and Max spoke to their agents. Laura emailed back that we are waiting for Max's agent to talk to him before they can start contacting the people who will get the script. So it still isn't officially going out this week.

FEBRUARY 23

7:00 A.M.
A text from Laura came in after I went to sleep last night:

> Max gave the sign off to send out the script. Will
> let you know when calls go out etc—of course
> aiming for this week.

It's now Wednesday. Aiming. I will need to be checked into a facility if it doesn't go out this week.

3:15 P.M.
I jumped rope at the Hudson River this morning. I could hear kids playing at the nearby water park. If I ever buy another house or apartment, I want it to be near a park so I can always hear kids playing, my favorite sound in the world.

I had a good meeting at noon with John and Kate. I am starting to get excited about their show.

I checked in with Laura at CAA and said I am sure if she aimed to achieve something, she could do it. Sadly, here is what she texted back:

> Yes, I am just waiting for Glenn and Max's team
> to advise on if they want to call any of the outlets
> and make sure I have appropriate bios for them,
> but otherwise I am ready to make calls. Just
> need to be mindful when dealing with all of these
> people and their reps.

I wrote back:

> Right. But since Max's agent requires a five-day
> delay for each step I assume then it is not going
> out this week. Oh well.

After a few more exchanges, Laura tried to give "good news":

> I already called my friend at Amazon about it who
> said it was a "fucking amazing package" and a
> "killer concept."

I wrote back:

> Thanks, I needed that.

Maybe someone will buy it. Doesn't really seem like an Amazon show to me, but I know nothing.

This is what Henry ate so far today:

* Breakfast: croissant
* Lunch: 2 slices of pizza
* Snack: cheese bread from Breads Bakery

This is my dream of what to eat in a day if I could. Maybe also a bagel with cream cheese and lettuce and tomato, which is actually what I did have this morning.

FEBRUARY 24

I tried to jump rope by the river again this morning, but it was much colder than yesterday.

There was an interesting development yesterday. Max Barbakow sent me this email at 4:30 p.m.:

> Glenn just called and pitched me Pete Davidson as Joey.
> They have a friendship I think and good chemistry. I think
> it's a pretty brilliant idea. What say you?

I texted back:

> Sure!

Glenn also emailed me saying Pete was a "friend" who she had "great chemistry with." I said I was excited by the idea of him doing the part, and within a couple of hours, Glenn forwarded an email from Pete that said he loved the idea and was "a million percent in."

Now, of course, he is a million percent in without having read the script. Max emailed back that we should send him a script. Glenn said she was going to have a call with Pete later that night and suggested that after she talked with him, Max and I should write him letters and then send him the script. I said I would, but I wondered how the script would get to him since I don't have his info.

Then a few hours later, I heard from Laura at CAA that Pete has another half hour he is committed to, which may not necessarily mean he can't do this one, but it certainly seems to be a complication, especially because that one hasn't gone to networks yet, and he may not be comfortable with ours going out first.

The night ended with an email from Glenn that said Pete was still shooting something, so they would talk today.

Christian, Glenn's manager, emailed this morning to say he was going to talk to Pete's reps about his other pilot commitment. I emailed back to ask if we were pausing on sending him a script and letters.

It's five o'clock and I never heard if Glenn talked to him, if I should write him a letter, and if he will be or was sent a script.

Henry loves the Louis Malle film *Vanya on 42nd Street*, so we walked up to the New Amsterdam Theatre, which is where it was shot. *Aladdin* is there now. We told the security guard in the lobby that Henry was a big fan of the movie and asked if we could take a look at the inside of the theater to see how different it looked now.

"I can't let anyone in," he said firmly, almost with anger. "It's a rule."

I understood, not assuming he would say yes. But on the other hand, it would be nice if the world didn't have firm rules.

"You look very nice and well-meaning," the security guard would say in this universe where rules weren't so firm. "Sure."

Then we would just pop our heads into the theater, look for a few seconds, and then get on with our day.

But we live in a world with firm rules. It's the world of the parking structure where you pay full price if you lose a ticket.

As we walked back down Seventh Avenue, my toes were numb from how cold it is. I forgot how cold toes can get in the winter.

It really made me remember how cold my toes would get when I would walk to and from school when I was a kid.

I'll finish what Henry had to eat yesterday:

* 1 piece of fresh bread when we visited my friend Michael in his new glamorous apartment that has made Henry question being a socialist
* 1 shrimp tostada and 1 buttered roll for dinner
* 1 slice of pizza after dinner at the pizza place in the opening credits of *Louie*
* 1 piece of chocolate babka for dessert

And this is what Henry had to eat so far today:

* 1 bagel with lox and cream cheese for a late breakfast
* 1 piece of pizza and 3 garlic knots for a late-afternoon snack

We are most likely having Chinese food for dinner, so he should be taking a break from any more bread today.

Also, Russia has invaded Ukraine. I am not sure what to think. I would normally read everything I can on a topic like this, but somehow my brain is only allowing me to read the headlines. The enormity of the horror is just too much.

FEBRUARY 25

It sounds really bad in Ukraine. It's such a scary, inhumane time. I am not sure what else to say, or think about. How can we be so lacking in figuring out a way for there to be better human rights internationally? Or nationally. What if human rights were something that was a class like history or English or math? Is it crazy to think that it would change something?

FEBRUARY 26

Eh, still upset and disoriented about Ukraine, but will give a quick recap of yesterday.

Glenn sent an email that said she texted Pete the script, and Max and I should email him letters ASAP. I was not home but said I would when I got home in a few hours.

Within an hour or two, Glenn sent an email that said Pete read the first eleven pages and wants to do it, which is quite something, since his character doesn't even show up until pages after that.

When I got back to our apartment, I wrote my letter to Pete telling him how excited I was when I imagined him in the part and how much I wanted to see him do it, and then sent it to him through Glenn. Glenn and I had a few emails back and forth, and she then wanted to give Pete my cell phone number for him to text me over the weekend, since he prefers texting to emailing.

There were various other emails from my agent and manager. Laura from CAA says Pete's agent is supportive of him doing the project, and the plan is for Glenn, Max, Pete, and myself to have a meeting Monday. But I talked to my manager, Ellyn, at the end of day, and we both agreed that we are still unsettled by this other half hour he is planning to go out with.

"Henry says he's never going to do it even though he says he is," I said.

"Why?" Ellyn asked.

"The agents," I said.

The real reason Ellyn was calling was to tell me Michael Showalter, a director who has a deal at HBO Max, is interested in hearing my pitch for an animated show. I pitched this idea in December to Netflix with producers who had a deal there, and the executive at Netflix seemed to be interested, but ultimately wasn't. So now I am tentatively scheduled to pitch it to Showalter's company sometime next week.

An assistant at CAA emailed that Glenn, Max, Pete, and I are to have a meeting at the beginning of next week. She is just waiting for Pete's people to give us a few times.

I have never seen Pete Davidson act in anything. So Henry and I watched him in a sketch from *Saturday Night Live*. I chuckled a few times. I liked him.

I went to bed. There was still no email with times for Pete, so I am assuming this meeting is not in fact happening Monday.

I woke up in the middle of the night and thought about checking my email.

But then I didn't, because whether there was or was not an email about Pete, I would be agitated and not be able to go back to sleep.

Now it's Saturday and we are on a flight back to Los Angeles. I just finished watching *Lady Boss*, a documentary about Jackie Collins. I had watched the first hour on the way to New York and found it pleasant, in a mildly distracting way. But the last hour was completely different—it was gripping and almost profound.

It was all because first, Jackie had this fun, great, exciting time when she was on top of the world, then had a tragic last act to her life. One of my greatest fears is to have a tragic last act.

I knew someone who did and would periodically think, Why doesn't he just do such and such to change his last act and make it less tragic? Or why doesn't he just do this other thing? Or another thing. But he didn't. He just had one long tragic last act. Which isn't even over by the way.

Part of me wishes I could write a Jackie Collins–like book. In the documentary, she makes it seems like such a fun life to have. She goes out to Hollywood parties and lunches and shops in Beverly Hills, then goes home and writes about what she has seen and heard.

I actually loved those type of books when I was a kid, especially the ones by Harold Robbins. Harold Robbins's sex scenes were so good and very informative if you had never had sex. I read a few Jackie Collins books when I was in my twenties, and they were much worse than Harold Robbins's books. A Jackie Collins book is a pretty dumb book.

The closest I came to writing one was when I was in my twenties and worked for the literary agent Irving Lazar. Mostly I just read his client's manuscripts for him and wrote a summary, as he rarely read anything. He called me up one day. Irving was famous for never saying "hello."

"Hey," he said as soon as I answered my phone. "Joan Collins has written a terrific novel. But she can't crack the first chapter."

"Okay," I said.

"So she is going to fax you the first chapter and you rewrite it and fax it back to her," he said.

"Okay," I said. Then he hung up.

A little later, Joan faxed a short prologue to her book, which was called *Love and Desire and Hate*, or something like that. The chapter was a little awkward, but it really wasn't that bad. It took me less than an hour to add a few sentences and change the order of a few pieces of information, then fax it back to her.

"Thanks," Irving said a day or two later. "Joanie loved what you did."

"It really wasn't much, honestly," I said.

"No, it was. You saved the day," Irving said. Irving was a lesson in how to make life more interesting. No one in Irving's life ever did something that wasn't much. People in Irving's life always did things that saved the day, even when they didn't. He had a wonderfully fun time living days that people always saved.

FEBRUARY 27

Henry bought a copy of *The Glass Menagerie* today with a cover featuring a beautiful drawing by Alvin Lustig. I just stared at it, as if I were in a museum. In fact, I was in the Guggenheim museum on Friday and stared less at the paintings in a Kandinsky exhibit. In fact, I practically jogged by the Kandinskys.

John just texted that he and Kate can't make the meeting we were supposed to have tomorrow morning. It's almost dinnertime on Sunday and Pete hasn't texted like Glenn said he would. I don't think he's going to.

Kirstie Alley was trending on Twitter, so sadly, I investigated why. It was because she tweeted something stupid about Ukraine. It made me think about her. I wondered what kind of person would hang out with a Kirstie Alley, and what those conversations would be like. It is not possible to have a less informed opinion than the opinions Kirstie Alley has. All her information is based not on facts or truth but on misinformation and conspiracy theories. So the idea of someone sitting with her, listening to her thoughts and then giving what has to be their equally less based in reality thoughts, boggles my mind. I would almost like to see a documentary about that. But then again, maybe I really wouldn't.

FEBRUARY 28

It's 11:30 a.m. No word yet on when this meeting with Pete Davidson is going to happen.

4:05 P.M.

Still no word. I was trying to jump rope outside, but a fly kept going in my ear. I am assuming it was the same fly again and again. Why would the fly be so intent on going in my ear? I gave up and will try again in a little while. Hopefully the fly won't still be there.

6:27 P.M.

The fly was still there. No word. I just emailed Ellyn to see if she has heard anything about Pete today.

MARCH 1

Ellyn emailed back that she hadn't heard anything last night. I asked her if I should contact Pete's manager to introduce myself. She said go for it and gave me his information. I sent him an email asking if we could have a short conversation today. I haven't heard back yet.

During the night I got an email from Evan, the producer attached to my New Zealand idea. It read:

> Hey Bruce!
>
> Happy to say Will is leaning in . . . He's mulling it but I'm hoping we can get into setting a Zoom sooner than later. Will report back asap.

In this case, I have a feeling ASAP means not for a while. Rob, my CAA agent, had a baby last week, and I am going to send him some children's books. I am trying to remember what are some unusual ones that I enjoyed reading to Henry and Eve that he might not know about. When they were little, I spent hours upon hours upon hours reading hundreds of picture books to them and in this moment, my mind is a complete blank, as if I just read them *Green Eggs and Ham* a couple of times.

I am having a hard time thinking while waiting for Pete to give a day and time for this meeting.

4:35 P.M.

An email came in that Pete is available to meet Friday morning. The script obviously isn't going to go out to people this week. I am assuming everyone is hoping Pete will attach to the project, which will help it sell. I'm a little nervous that I will read Sigourney Weaver and Chris Holland (whoever that is) are in a pilot that everyone wanted that sold to HBO Max before this goes out.

I just told Kate about the meeting with Pete, and she smiled with delight. I wish I could be excited instead of always wondering when the other shoe will drop.

"You have PTSD," Kate said, referring to all the times I have been told something was going to happen and then it didn't.

I nodded. I do have PTSD.

Now we are waiting to watch Biden's State of the Union speech. I have been able to turn on the television ever since I got the lesson from Henry, so I guess the lesson actually did work.

MARCH 2

There was an Emergency Alert test on the radio this morning and Kate thought it was an actual Emergency Alert. It made me think, one day it won't be a test. What will our emergency be? Also, once we hear the alert, what exactly are we going to do? All drive somewhere else? What will that look like? It seems like it might be the worst traffic jam ever.

I guess I am freaked out by what is happening in Ukraine, plus Biden's speech. He did a great job, but by the end, he had listed about five hundred things that he was going to fix. So many things need to be fixed. It's like this house. Everything needs to be fixed. I don't remember a time where there were this many things to fix. And what about all the things we need to fix that he didn't even mention?

I should be looking over my notes for the animated show today in preparation for pitching it tomorrow. I just can't bring myself to. I'm agitated by the world and exhausted from the *Hindenburg* pace of trying to sell a TV show. So I am not going to look at my notes. It's more of a laundry/cleaning/making chickpea tuna salad day.

12:20 P.M.

I needed to make vegan mayonnaise for the chickpea tuna salad and I always make vegan Caesar dressing on the vegan mayonnaise days, so I ended up making the mayonnaise, then the dressing, then the chickpea tuna salad.

As I was making the dressing, "Spiegel im Spiegel" by Arvo Pärt came on the classical music station. It's one of my favorites. It translates to "Mirror in the Mirror." I have no idea what "Mirror in the Mirror" means, but it is exactly what the music sounds like. It gave me such a lift. It's a reminder that there is art too in this world, and art is just as real, or more real, than all the things that need fixing.

Pete has to change the meeting to the afternoon on Friday. I said I could do that. I'm doubtful both Glenn and Max will be able to do it. Now I'm starting to sink a little bit.

So I am going to play "Rhyme of Another Summer" by Yann Tierson on YouTube. which I always do when I need a lift. It really works.

6:39 P.M.

Max and Glenn can do the new time. Clearly, if both of them can switch to the new time, I think we can safely say that Pete is very, very big.

MARCH 3

I saw the man whose phone I stole at the gym today. He still hates me. He glared at me very angrily as I was going in the elevator and he was getting out.

When I got in the car this morning, the steering wheel had an unfamiliar shake, as if it suddenly got Parkinson's. I called the car place and scheduled an appointment for tomorrow to see if it actually is Parkinson's. I mean, part of me knows it isn't Parkinson's, but part of me doesn't know that.

I have to pitch the animated idea in two hours. This is the part of the job I really hate.

6:08 P.M.

The animated pitch meeting was short. I was done in thirty-seven minutes. But it seemed to go as well as it possibly could.

At the beginning of the meeting, Michael Showalter's development person asked me how I was.

"I'm fine," I said. "But the world isn't."

We talked about how scary everything is for the first few minutes, then Michael came on and we talked about various places we could all move to—Canada, Portugal, Iceland, all the usual suspects.

"We can all get jobs in Iceland," Michael said. "I hear there are tons of jobs."

"Really?" I said.

"Yes," he said. "They need cabdrivers."

"Oh," I said, not really sure that I would like to be a cabdriver. "Can't we just do this animated show from Iceland? All my friends on animated shows never have to leave their houses since the pandemic. It's very doable."

Then I went into the pitch.

Michael was very encouraging during it and seemed to understand and like the idea. He had a few questions to clarify things like tone but didn't register any hesitations or concerns.

He asked me if I needed to know more about his company, but I said I didn't. I explained that I had chosen to pitch to them because they had a deal with HBO Max, which is my target for this idea. But more important, I wanted to work with him specifically because I thought he was the right fit for my sensibility, and he agreed.

"Great," he said.

At the end of the meeting, Michael said, "This idea is all that I hoped it would be." Which is a very nice thing to hear.

I went into the living room after. "How did it go?" Kate asked.

"They seem to want to do it," I said.

"Great," she said.

"I don't want to do this anymore," I said. She nodded, totally understanding.

After a minute she said, "I don't want to do this anymore either. I've spent all day doing unpaid work." She was referring to a project she is considering. It's an adaptation of a book for a limited series, and she was preparing for her second meeting on the project with the producers.

I left to go pick up Henry from school.

"I pitched the animated show to a new producer," I said to him. "It seemed to go well."

"It always goes well," he said. "Then nothing ever happens."

"True," I said.

MARCH 4

It's Pete Davidson day. I went to the car place in Santa Monica at 7:00 a.m. and dropped off the car.

"It should be ready by ten thirty," the man at the car place said. I then got a lift to the gym. I was there for a long time. At ten, the man at the car place texted it would just be a little longer than expected.

At eleven, I got on the Metro train to go to Santa Monica. On the train, the man texted that I needed new tires and that meant they needed to be aligned and then asked would it be okay to pick up at three. I texted back:

No

I have a meeting at two which I have to be home for

I had already said this to him when I dropped the car off.

He then said the car could be ready by 1:30 p.m. It made me a little nervous about what kind of work they would do in a rush, but I agreed. Especially because I need to be able to drive the car down to Orange County this weekend for Eve's volleyball club.

Now I was on my way to Santa Monica for no reason. I got off and walked around Santa Monica. That is all I did for hours. I barely had any thoughts. I was just waiting for the meeting with Pete.

Santa Monica was depressing—so many closed stores, and so many sad and/or angry people who were seemingly living on the streets. I talked to several of them. Or rather they tried to talk to me, and I tried to be friendly without engaging with them.

Finally at one o'clock, I went to the car place. I wanted to make myself a visible presence. The car wasn't ready. It was on its second realignment. I was starting to get very nervous. But then they said it was ready, and I was home before the meeting, which was actually at two fifteen.

The meeting was short. But I liked Pete, and he was very enthusiastic and said he definitely wants to do the show. He indicated he would prefer to do it before his other show. He is shooting a movie in the summer, so we talked about our show shooting in the fall.

"I can definitely have all the scripts ready by then," I said.

Glenn's manager was in the meeting and said the script would go out next Thursday and everyone was good with that.

I am oddly numb about it all and strangely tired. I feel like Jane Fonda in *They Shoot Horses, Don't They?* She played a woman in a 1930s dance marathon. I saw it when I was a kid and was horrified by the desperation and exhaustion of the people in *They Shoot Horses, Don't They?* Actually, even though the movie would be classified as a drama, I sat there in my parents' house experiencing it like a horror film. I never wanted to end up like Jane Fonda in *They Shoot Horses, Don't They?* and somehow now I have.

I feel like I am not quite done pushing this rock up a hill although perhaps the top of the hill is finally in sight.

MARCH 5

I got up at five thirty to take Eve to the volleyball tournament in Orange Country. Volleyball tournament days are long days.

I thought about Glenn and Pete and the project, and for the first time, I thought, this might actually happen.

MARCH 6

I've been thinking a lot about winning and losing today. I just won a game of Ping-Pong with Henry. We play about twenty games a week. And maybe I win one game every two weeks and he wins thirty-nine games every two weeks.

"It's not fun to never win," I said to him, upset, about two months ago, after losing yet another game.

He looked at me, genuinely confused. I think he might have

been wondering if he should let me win sometimes, the way you let a little kid win sometimes, although I have no memory of actually doing that when the kids were little. Maybe I didn't.

Anyway, ever since I said it's not fun to never win, I have actually been able to have fun never winning. It's strange how that works sometimes. You say what your reality is, and that allows you to have a different reality. At least that is the case for me.

Some days, I am in the backyard losing to Henry, and it is the highlight of my day. I appreciate being in what I consider to be a beautiful space in the beautiful California light that I will miss when I move one day. And there is something so relaxing about being outside on a nice day, hearing the quiet sounds coming from nearby backyards in our neighborhood. And in those moments, I don't care about whether I win or lose. I just like doing what I am doing with who I am doing it with.

Eve's volleyball team lost a few games yesterday. Their final game was close. As they started to fall behind, one of the other player's fathers started getting louder and louder with his yells encouraging them. He is always very vocal, but now he was even more vocal than usual.

"One game," he screamed. "One game." He was clearly trying to say, come on, all you have to do is get a few more points, and you can with this. "One game! One game!"

Then they lost and he was quiet. We started to get our things together to all go. None of the parents were talking, but he seemed the most quiet.

I was once playing Monopoly when I was a kid. I can't remember who I was playing with, but as soon as one of the other kids sensed he was going to lose and have to leave the game, he promptly overturned the board, and all the pieces and money went flying. Now no one could win. I wish I could remember who the person was, but I just can't. I'm scared it was me, even though I know it wasn't.

Putin feels like that kid. The news out of Ukraine is so scary. It just feels like Putin is about to overturn the Monopoly board and everything is going to go flying.

I wonder if this Glenn-and-now-Pete project is making me think about winning, because finally, I might win. I mean, in terms of getting a television show made. I have written more pilots than anyone else I know and never had my own show. I wrote my first pilot over three decades ago and have written something like three dozen pilots. That is a lot of not winning.

On the other hand, when I am in my right mind, I know that I have won. I get to lose at Ping-Pong with Henry every day. I get to watch Eve lose at volleyball. And I get to lose a fight with Kate. There is no other person I would rather lose a fight to than Kate.

When I was a kid, I loved when Tevye said something like, "On the other other hand" in *Fiddler on the Roof*, so I am going to say it now.

On the other other hand, is it easier to be in our right mind or your highest self when at least there is the hope of winning? And is that where I am in this moment?

I do have hope in this moment, which I know there has not been a lot of lately.

MARCH 7

I had a vegetable peeler I loved. Over twenty-five years ago, I took over a rent-controlled apartment from a friend, with the under-standing he might want it back some day. Some of his things were still in the apartment. When he died a few years later, I inherited the few things he had left in the apartment. One of them was an old very simply designed vegetable peeler. It was the perfect object. Kate strangely never liked the vegetable peeler. She just couldn't work it for some reason, so after she moved into my house, she bought a new vegetable peeler. So she had hers and I had mine, which as I said already, but can't stress enough, I loved.

About six weeks ago, her vegetable peeler disappeared. Since she can't work mine, she bought a new one. Then three weeks ago, my vegetable peeler also disappeared. We both blame Henry, who never puts anything back in the right place.

I searched and searched and searched for my vegetable peeler. I used to put it in a spot in the utensil drawer near where all the measuring spoons go. So I went through all the measuring spoons because that would be the natural place for it to be hidden.

It wasn't there. I looked everywhere in the kitchen, then went back to the measuring spoons. It still wasn't there.

I would look for it periodically, and anytime I needed to peel something, I used Kate's new vegetable peeler, which I hate.

About a week ago, I finally stopped looking for it, assumed it had been thrown out accidentally, and accepted my new life with the bad peeler.

Then last night, as I was looking for a measuring spoon, there it was in the measuring spoon place. I have chills as I type this.

It was pure magic. And even more important, if my vegetable peeler came back, it means there is still magic in this world.

It can't just be the peeler. It means magic can happen at any moment.

Henry has been listening to a lot of ELO music lately. ELO is Electric Light Orchestra, a group no one ever references from my youth. I love ELO too, but Henry listens to the same three ELO songs over and over again on our car trips to and from school, so I suggested he go to their greatest hits album so we could hear new ones.

He found one called "Strange Magic." I didn't recognize the title, but when it started playing, I remembered it. It was fun to hear it after all these years. I find the title interesting. I would have said that all magic is strange. But maybe ELO knows more than

I do—some magic is strange magic. The vegetable peeler coming back was very strange and special magic for me.

MARCH 8

It was a Silent Monday yesterday. John and Kate have disappeared since they canceled our meeting a week ago. Evan hasn't emailed with an update on Will Forte for the New Zealand idea. I never heard anything from Showalter's people about the animated show.

And the biggest silence was not hearing anything about the Glenn and Pete show. On Friday, Laura from CAA said that she would talk to Pete's people yesterday or today to confirm that the script will go out to people later this week.

As I think I said once, but will say again, when you don't hear anything on Monday, the silence feels even more silent than when you don't hear anything on other work days.

In terms of Ukraine, I just saw a headline that the threat of nuclear weapons is increasing. I am not sure how to think or even just go about my day during this time.

Plus, Henry brushed his teeth with sunscreen this morning.

Eve is on spring break. I drove her to volleyball club practice in Santa Barbara yesterday. As we were driving home late at night, we listened to a little disco music. "Doctor's Orders" by Carol Douglas, one of my favorite disco songs, was playing.

"Did you go to disco parties?" Eve asked.

"I think I went to actual discos," I said. Although now that I think about it, maybe I just went to clubs that sometimes played disco music.

She was quiet for a moment.

"You got to live through such fun periods," she said quietly. And sadly. "No climate change."

"No," I said. "We just had pollution." She was quiet once again.

12:57 P.M.

Ellyn emailed that she texted with Laura who said she is scheduled to speak to Ayala, Pete's agent, at 5:00 p.m. Also she said she owes Showalter's development person a call. So it's just a waiting day.

MARCH 9

So it's not great. Laura spoke with Ayala, who maybe is Pete's manager. Or maybe agent. I am not sure. I thought Ayala was a woman, but I think Laura referred to her as he, so maybe Ayala is a man. Ayala had to be circumspect for two reasons—one is that Pete is getting death threats. Not sure why that has to do with anything but let's put that aside. The other reason is that Pete wasn't supposed to tell us his other show is with Amazon. That information was secret. Amazon is supposed to announce that show today, and then Laura can talk again to Ayala and Ayala will be more forthcoming with all the information. But Ayala did say that show is supposed to shoot before he would shoot another show such as mine.

However, Pete did say he was in charge of what would shoot when, and he wants to do mine first, so perhaps he can shoot mine first.

The biggest problem is that if his show is being announced today, we can't go out with the script this week. Laura felt we would have to wait at least another week before going out with another Pete Davidson show.

After I talked to her, I wondered if it would help to present mine as a limited series, a show with only one season, which after all is how Pete thought of it in the first place. I discussed this with Ellyn, and she thought maybe that would allow us to still go out with the script this week.

But it is definitely looking like this path is far from likely.

If I step back, I know it is good that I still have Pete. But I am slightly going mad from being told over and over that this script is going out next week and then it never does. And by slightly going mad, I mean really going mad.

Laura also reported that Glenn wants Christian to be a producer and asked how I felt about that.

"Great," I said. "I would love to have him as a producer." To me, that seems like a good idea, but, of course, I could be wrong.

12:21 P.M.

The day is half over and still no announcement from Amazon about Pete's other show. Kate Berlant just texted that she and John are busy with their special for Peacock, so the meeting we were supposed to have about ten days ago will be sometime after March 29, which is about three weeks from now. I am still waiting to hear about the animated idea, and naturally haven't heard a word about the New Zealand idea. On the way to school this morning, I was on the highway and got stuck behind an enormous truck going very, very slowly. I pulled out of the lane and passed him and then moments later was behind yet another enormous truck going very, very slowly. In our neighborhood there has been tons of construction, and I have noticed that the trucks have gotten bigger and slower and there are more of them. I feel like I am permanently behind an extremely enormous truck going very slowly. The question is, is there any way I can learn to enjoy it?

3:47 P.M.

I was just out in the world. It's a lot of human suffering-on-the-street day.

Still no announcement from Amazon. If there is no announcement, then what?

5:15 P.M.

The announcement came, although strangely it did not mention Amazon. It just said that the show was set up and the deal was being "finalized." Max forwarded an email from his agent saying we should wait to go out until next week. I said I wasn't sure that was for the best but would do what the group wants.

Ellyn thinks we should go out with it this week. Laura wants to talk to Ayala, who is now officially a woman.

MARCH 10

Laura emailed at 7:15 a.m. to get an updated logline of the script and to double-check that she has the latest draft, both of which needed to be updated to reflect Pete's age. These two requests would seem to indicate that the script is going out today. I would have thought I would feel elated, but instead I am filled with dread and have an enormous weight on my chest.

Here is the logline I sent her:

Glenn Close and Pete Davidson star in the story of Nora Merman, a divorced mother of adult children who falls in love with Joey Vacarella, a man almost half a century younger than her, altering her life and the lives of those around her.

Then a half hour later, I had a thought for another line to put at the end and sent this:

Glenn Close and Pete Davidson star in the story of Nora Merman, a divorced mother of adult children who falls in love with Joey Vacarella, a man almost half a century younger than her, altering her life and the lives of those around her.

Maybe, just maybe, love does conquer all.

11:00 A.M.

I just had a phone call with Ellyn. I thought it was going to be about the Glenn/Pete project. But it was about Showalter's company and the animated idea.

"They loved you," she said. "But they don't want to move forward."

She then explained that they felt it skewed too old for HBO Max and they didn't like the fact that the word "death" was in the title and the subject matter of the show, although really it is about life, not death, of course. She kept saying "they" over and over again.

"It's not they," I said. "It's Jordana." That's Showalter's development person. "He loved the idea. She thinks HBO Max won't buy it. And she may be right. But he didn't seem to think that at all."

Ellyn disagreed with my perception, but I said I felt I had more information, being the person who was there on the Zoom. In any case, it is quite a surprise and disappointment.

I walked into Kate's office when I hung up with Ellyn and told her.

"I feel like I should just stop doing this," I said. "It is crazy for me to keep doing this. Jordana is probably right that HBO Max would never want this. They want season two of *Minx*."

Our friend Cara is up for a job on season two of *Minx*, so we watched the trailer for season one the other day. It was one of the most awful things I have ever seen. And I have seen a lot of awful things.

I then got an email from Laura. The Glenn/Pete script is officially going out next week. But, of course, since I have been told that every week for the last five weeks, I am not assuming it is going to go out next week, or ever.

I just had a really dark thought. Whatever I want to do, no network or streamer wants to do. If by some miracle this script gets bought and made, it will not be because of the script that I wrote. It will be despite the script that I wrote. They want *Minx*, they don't want this script. I had to get Glenn then Max then Pete to have someone buy this script.

It really is crazy that I keep doing this. It's the definition of insanity. I thought that this journal was about me trying to get a television show bought and made. But what if it's the opposite? Maybe this journal is about learning to stop hitting my head against a wall. Maybe it is about me finding a new life doing something completely different that I love. Maybe, just maybe, love does conquer all.

MARCH 11

There is an expression I always loved. I have no idea when I first heard it. Maybe it was when I first moved to Los Angeles when I was twenty-one. Or maybe it was in my childhood.

"The phone stopped ringing," someone would say, usually about someone else. It would be said in a sad tone of voice, and it meant the jobs stopped coming. Whoever it was said about was now just in their house, out of work, sitting quietly.

I feel like this book might end up with the title *The Phone Stopped Ringing* or, of course, it could always be called *The Phone Started Ringing*, if anything does come along.

I mean, I know the phone is still ringing, so to speak, but it doesn't feel that way.

The phone is definitely not ringing today. I was just in the backyard jumping rope and it was very silent. I tried enjoying the silence.

And then a jackhammer started somewhere a few houses away. The sound of a jackhammer is one of my two least favorite sounds. The other one is opera. Opera makes me want to kill myself.

I tried enjoying the sound of the distant jackhammer and was moderately successful. Especially when I thought to myself, a jack-hammer is a lot better than hearing the sound of a bomb, which is what people in Ukraine are hearing.

Now I will go around the house looking for things to clean. I have to go to the hardware store later to get some shower cleaning supplies. I hate going to the hardware store because it always feels so MAGA in there.

4:47 P.M.

I just cleaned all the windows in the living room. They're crystal clear. I'm scared about what's going to happen with the birds.

MARCH 12

"I'm discombobulated," my mother often said when I was a child. I don't know why I thought of that this morning. Maybe because I have been discombobulated often lately, especially since 2016.

That's seven years of discombobulation, seven years of feeling like a child in the back seat of a car being driven by an out-of-control angry, stupid drunk driver. Even after Biden got elected, new out-of-control stupid drunk drivers came forward, so even if he is calm and sober, he is driving on the road with these people. And now we all have to deal with Putin on the road.

Literally, we have spent the last month having to deal with the creepy truckers making insane convoys on the road in various countries. And just this morning, I read another article about the likelihood of civil war in this country due to democracy being in jeopardy and identity politics.

Henry and I watched *Saboteur* last night. It's one of the Alfred Hitchcock movies I have the most fondness for. When it would show up on TV when I was a kid, I would be very excited.

There is something about it that just grips me. I know that Robert Cummings and Priscilla Lane are technically not considered very good actors, but in this movie they are good. In fact, they are both extremely good. I think it is because they both lead with their pain. He, of course, is also good in *Dial M for Murder*, which I could see once a year always, if not more.

There is something very sad about the journey across the country that they go on together in *Saboteur*. I hadn't seen it in over forty years but watched it over and over again back then, so I had a strange experience watching it this time. Every time I encountered a new scene, it was a surprise, and yet I then instantly remembered it.

Oh, right, this happens, I thought to myself, practically grinning with delight.

This happened to me when they happened upon a train of circus freaks. It's such a beautiful and unique scene, about one billion times better than the Guillermo del Toro remake of *Nightmare Alley* that our friend Nicole made Kate and I see part of.

At various points, the couple in the film reach out to strangers to help them, and just when it looks like they aren't going to get it, they find one person who will help them.

"This movie is about how you just need to find one good person," Henry said.

I nodded that he was right.

"Every time they need to find a good person, they do," he said. "There are just enough good people in the world."

11:25 A.M.

I was thinking of a friend's mother this morning and how she never does anything. She doesn't load a dishwasher or sweep a floor or even just put a single flower in a vase. She just watches television and puts a cup of coffee someone bought for her the day before or two days before in a microwave.

It seems sad to me to never do anything for yourself. If I could, I would do everything for myself.

It's been almost exactly two years since I stopped drawing cartoons, and I miss it sometimes, but not enough to start doing them again. I used to think of it as part of who I was, and now I think of it as part of who I was but not who I am.

MARCH 13

It's Sunday. I woke up at seven thirty this morning and wondered why I slept so late. I meditated and wrote my morning pages and read the paper and cleaned. Kate came out at nine.

"Why did you sleep so late?" I asked her.

"It's daylight savings time," she said.

I had been told that yesterday but of course forgot. And because my phone and computer changed the time on their own, I hadn't been confronted with the wrong time. It made me miss how it used to be.

The *New York Times* (which now I see only online) had a clock in the bottom left-hand corner of the front page on Saturday to remind you about daylight savings time. And then the next day, you would wander around the house, changing all the times of the little clocks on tables and desks or the big clock on the wall.

Daylight savings time is so strange because it is like you get to decide time. You can lose an hour or you can gain an hour. But on the other hand, it's an illusion. Time really decides what time is. And ultimately, when time decides it's your time, time wins.

We went to a birthday party yesterday for a one-year-old. She's my friend Sarah's daughter, Juniper. Sarah is exactly twenty years younger than me.

The party was full of Sarah's friends, mostly the same age as she is, many with kids under the age of four. I don't think that I wished

I could be their age. But part of me does wish our kids were that age, so maybe part of me does.

"You're going to be my first friend to die," Sarah said to me one day when we were sitting on the set of *Girls*.

"Maybe not," I said.

"Maybe," she said, clearly not convinced. On another day, not that long after, I looked over at her and said, "That's a good look for my funeral." I think it was the same look that we referred to as her "Radzi" look, because she looked like Carole Radziwill from *Real Housewives of New York*.

One day Sarah was talking about *Law & Order: SVU* and I said I never watched it because it was too disturbing for me.

"People your age say that," she said.

"Like who?" I asked.

She looked at me. "My mother," she said.

"Your mother is not my age," I said. I was upset but really not. We both laughed.

Her mother was at the party yesterday. She's now seventy, I think. I talked to her for a long time. Maybe because she actually is my age.

I know that a little later, when I told Kate Sarah's mother's age, Kate was shocked. Kate thought she must be much older.

And it was not because she looked older. She actually looks very young. Kate was just not thinking about how much younger Sarah is than us, and is used to thinking of our parents' friends as being in their eighties, usually.

Kate looked a little disturbed. "She's almost our age," she said.

"No, she isn't," I said.

"Well, she's closer to our age than the people at this party that are Sarah's age," she said.

"That's true," I said. I looked away from the party and studied a couple on a basketball court happily running after their four-year-old and was somehow sad. Time always wins.

MARCH 14

I dropped Henry off at school and went to the dentist to have my teeth cleaned. I always leave the dentist thoroughly exhausted by the mere act of having to keep my mouth open for an hour.

Do other people find it more exhausting to keep your mouth open for an hour than to exercise, I wonder every time I go to the dentist.

Afterward, I got an email from Laura at CAA:

> Hey Bruce—good morning! Wanted to let you know that Ellyn, Rob, and I are circling up with everyone and getting synced up with a finalized plan (the goal is to take it out this week). We'll call you or email you as soon as we have more. Very excited!

I wrote back:

> When you say "goal," is it likely to not go out this week?

She replied:

> I put everyone on a chain (Ellyn, Rob, Ben—Glenn's CAA agent, Christian, Lauren—Max's agent, and Ayala—Pete's agent) to get the ball rolling on making submissions this week. I have no reason (at the moment) to believe there will be a holdup!

But, of course, since it's Monday there is still plenty of time for a holdup.

I woke up this morning and thought everything is an opportunity. So I am trying not to be attached to any outcome. I am not sure how well I am going to succeed at that.

Kate bought something called Gorilla Glue to fix a blind in her office. I borrowed it and used it to fix a little ceramic bunny Eve made when she was younger. The bunny came from a mold, so it is not as if she actually made it. She just colored it. But the colors are so pleasing to my eye and I think of her painting it when I look at it. It broke years ago and I keep it on a shelf. The bunny's head is in three pieces, but if I put them together and point the head against the wall, the bunny appears to not be broken. Occasionally if I touch the shelf, the bunny's head falls apart. Today that happened and I realized I could use Kate's glue to really fix the bunny's head.

The bunny means nothing to Eve or to anyone other than me. It's like my vegetable peeler. This house is filled with little things here and there that only have meaning for one person in this whole universe.

I am trying to be in touch with the fact that the broken bunny and the vegetable peeler are what's real, not whether this script sells or even goes out to anyone.

3:20 P.M.

I had a couple of thoughts.

It feels like Eve liked me better when she was younger. I understand that this is my fear, rather than the actual truth, but, like all my fears, it feels true. Perhaps that is why I am so attached to the broken bunny and the other remnants of her younger self that I have put in the living room and laundry area.

All my other projects seem stalled or dead. No New Zealand, no animated show, no Kate and John. And no TV shows that I would want to do are asking if I would go on staff. So this Glenn/ Pete project seems like the last boat out for me. It's this project or just doing something else for my work life.

5:17 P.M.

Just sitting here waiting for the business day to end. If it does and I haven't heard anything from Laura or Ellyn, it means Pete is still in and nothing has happened to make the script not go out this week.

MARCH 15

I had to drive Eve up to Santa Barbara for her volleyball club practice. Before we went, I was annoyed by the idea of the two-hour drive up, then the two-hour practice, then the two-hour drive back. If I am going to Santa Barbara, I prefer to hang out there for longer and I resented driving up at the time of day when it takes the longest to get there.

However, Eve and I drove the back way up the Pacific Coast Highway. And the time of day that it takes the longest also includes the sunset, the most beautiful time of the day. And Eve and I had a nice conversation for most of the ride. I really enjoyed being with her and felt she enjoyed being with me. It really made me happy. So what I thought I didn't want was actually what was most right for me. I am constantly relearning this. So I am sure I will only hold on to this thought for a moment, then forget it.

While she was playing volleyball, I got this email from Laura:

Hey!

Ayala (Pete's agent) approved the list to start making calls this week:

Amazon: Ryan Andolina, Alix Taylor Apple: Matt Cherniss,
Dana Tuinier Netflix: Tracey Pakosta, Andy Weil Peacock: Jeff
Meyerson

HBO: Amy Gravitt, Allie Wasserman

HBO Max: Suzanna Makkos, Billy Wee Hulu: Jordan Helman, Billy
Rosenberg FX: Kate Lambert, Kevin Wandell

Paramount+: Nicole Clemens, Jana Helman Showtime: Amy
Israel, Jessie Dicovitsky

We will keep you posted on this chain when we have submitted
to each one.

Thanks!

Ellyn, Rob, and Laura

So not only did no bad news happen by the end of the business day,
it seems we have moved a step forward to the script going out this week.

This list is not unfamiliar, as I first got that other version of it over
a month ago, that first week the script was going to go out then didn't.

I find it strange to be a girls' volleyball club dad. There is one
dad who screams millions of things at the girls for hours and hours
at the tournaments. I could never scream at someone to win a point.
Or scream that she won a point. Or scream to keep trying to get a
point. Kate can, which I find interesting.

All the parents would prefer that Kate be there than me. No
one knows what to do with me. And I always seem to say the wrong
thing whenever anyone engages with me.

At the last tournament, Eve's team was twelve points ahead of the team they were playing.

I turned to the mother next to me and said, "This is crazy, isn't? They're so ahead!"

Moments later, they promptly started losing point after point until the other team ultimately got ahead. Now they were losing.

The mother turned to me.

"You jinxed it," she said, annoyed.

2:32 P.M.

Laura emailed that she spoke to Netflix and they have now been sent the script. It's actually happening.

6:27 P.M.

Laura emailed that now half of the places have been spoken to, and sent scripts. The places that don't have it yet are Amazon, HBO, HBO Max, Peacock, and Showtime.

I have been in the kitchen for hours making croutons, chickpea tuna salad, vegan mayonnaise, and vegan Caesar dressing.

Now I'm going back to the kitchen to start working on dumplings and onion pancakes from Trader Joe's.

I said to Kate, "If no one buys it, then do I just leave the business?"

"Maybe," she said.

MARCH 16

Minx is getting all good reviews. One hundred percent on Rotten Tomatoes. I am not sure what else there is to say about that.

My friend Nicole wanted to talk yesterday and I offered her a few times, but she never got back to me. Today she texted:

Sorry. The day got away from me.

"The day got away from me" is one of my favorite expressions. I wish I was having a day that got away from me. Currently I am stuck with my day all day long.

I got a haircut this morning. The person who cut my hair was from Kansas. He said he left there because he didn't like living there. I asked why.

"They don't like anyone who is different from them," he said. He clearly felt different from them. "I don't blame them. Everyone there is the same."

He went on to say how much he liked living in Los Angeles because everyone was different from each other. Later, I thought to myself, but he was in Kansas, and he was different from them. So everyone there is not the same. They just make the ones who are different feel bad about being different. So bad that they want to leave.

I would like to say something about tribalism here. When I am in my highest self, I am in touch with the fact that we are all one. And I desperately pray for the time that all of us know that all the time, or more than we do now.

During my haircut, there were disturbing reports from Ukraine on the news. I understand why people feel it is racist to get more upset about this invasion than other invasions.

But I would like to offer another thought on this. The other invasions seem to happen in more overtly chaotic places. The people living in Ukraine seemed to be living in a country with more order. Of course, that was an illusion. And it brings up the fact that all order is possibly an illusion, which is not a fun thought.

So I am trying to accept the chaos today. It is all chaos and I am grateful to be having a day with at least the illusion of order.

MARCH 17

Laura sent an email at the end of yesterday that Amazon, HBO, and HBO Max now have the script. It still hasn't been sent to Peacock and Showtime. I never watch anything on Peacock or Showtime, so I'm definitely not interested in what they think of the project.

I somehow have the vague sense that it is not going well. It is instinctive. But hopefully I am wrong.

At the gym this morning, I heard a familiar song, but couldn't quite place it and couldn't quite hear the lyrics. It reminded me of being in my twenties. It made me think of a weekend meal I once had at a restaurant in Santa Monica that doesn't exist anymore. I was there with my friend Willie and some other guys he and I used to hang out with. We were all single, all just starting out in our careers or the careers we were trying to have but didn't have yet, excited by what we hoped and maybe assumed would come. My energy then was so much lighter than it is today. Everything was possible then as opposed to now, when everything seems impossible.

I went up to Dan, the man who works behind the desk at the gym, and asked, "Can I ask you who sings this song?"

"Arcade Fire," he said. I had expected him to need to look at the computer, but he didn't.

"You just know that off the top of your head?" I asked, stunned because he is decades younger than me and I assumed they were just some one-hit wonder band from the 1980s.

"Yes," he said. "I don't know most of the music we play. I just happen to know the band."

Later, as I was leaving, Dan asked, "Did you like the song or hate it?"

"I liked it," I said. "It reminded me of the 1980s. Is it from 1986 or 1987, something like that?"

"It's from five years ago," he said. "But it does have an 1980s sound."

I was taken aback. It is as if I had a false recovered memory.

"I'm going to go home and listen to it again," I said. I didn't even ask the name of the song because I was so sure they only had one hit. Now I am home and they have song after song after song and song and I can't find the one that was playing at the gym.

I'll ask Dan what it was tomorrow.

I don't know what to do with myself, so I am going to make vegan broccoli soup even though I know Eve and her friend Sophie Saxl, who is staying with us, will not eat it.

7:58 P.M.

Laura just emailed:

> We are officially out to everyone—here we go!!

Not sure that we are actually going anywhere, but sure.

MARCH 18

Eve had the broccoli soup, but Sophie Saxl didn't. And Dan told me the name of the song when I asked him at the gym.

"'Everything Now,'" he said with a smile.

When I got home later, I put the original video for it on YouTube. It didn't sound right.

The person who was singing sounded like he was in a severe depression and was saying something seemingly about not being able to get out of a dark place. Instead of being upbeat, it was all so slow and depressing.

Oh great, I thought, of course Dan didn't give me the right name. The singer continued on, practically moaning something else bleak. Definitely not the right song, I thought. This song is awful.

And then magically, the song turned into the upbeat melodic anthem it is. The wrong song turned into the right song.

Something bad turned into something good.

Everything now. That's a lot. Everything now seems so bad. I was just listening to Kathy Griffin talking to Kara Swisher on her podcast. I knew Kathy very, very slightly a million years ago.

They were talking about cancel culture and then politics. Kathy is clearly a great critical thinker and she was discussing the midterms this year and the presidential election in 2024 and what is happening today with Florida and Texas, with the rights of trans people. It's so scary how casually we are now talking about the possibility of authoritarian rule in the United States not just being possible, but in some ways likely.

So this morning I have come up with an escape plan. When I was in New Zealand, I looked for a turkey sandwich everywhere. No one had turkey sandwiches, but I kept looking. On Thanksgiving, the set caterers served a special but strange brown turkey for me and the seven other Americans working far from home. Months later, back in America, I found out it had actually been chicken.

When I came back from New Zealand, I was ravenous for turkey sandwiches and I still am. I basically only want to eat turkey sandwiches and pizza, but force myself to eat other things.

So my escape plan is . . . to bring turkey sandwiches to New Zealand. I will get some turkeys shipped there and have a turkey farm where I humanely raise turkeys and give them a long life until they are ready to become turkey sandwiches. I'm not sure Kate is going to go for this. Or if New Zealand is either.

But I am now an expert on turkey sandwiches and feel very confident I could make turkey sandwiches people would want.

If this script doesn't sell, then I am definitely going to explore becoming a turkey farmer in New Zealand.

"Maybe we should just move to the country and buy a farm," my father would say when I was a kid.

We would all roll our eyes because it seemed the most unlikely thing to ever happen. But maybe I should move to New Zealand and have my turkey farm as a salute to my father.

But until I make my getaway, my goal is to enjoy the life that I have now amidst the horror that is happening in the world.

How do we enjoy our time while fighting the growing racism and authoritarianism far away and right in our backyard?

If this Glenn/Pete project happens, I want to explore how to enjoy the moment because this moment is all that is real. And by this moment, I do mean this exact one.

I have the tiniest Kathy Griffin story. It's something that Willie told me, but like many of the things he told me, I almost feel like they happened to me.

He went to a party that Kathy gave. It was before she was that successful. She lived in a tiny apartment in somewhere like Beachwood Canyon, I think. He said that there weren't that many people at the party and it was sort of depressing and Kathy was in the middle of the tiny apartment, just dancing by herself.

But now I wonder, maybe Kathy was just enjoying the moment, dancing by herself and not caring who was there or not there or not dancing with her. I like to think she was.

MARCH 19

I've been reading *Agee on Film* before I go to bed. It's the most relaxing book. It's a collection of James Agee's film reviews from the *Nation* and maybe some other publication and they are unlike any other movie reviews. Instead of giving formal synopses of the plot and assessments of each actor and the writing and the directing, he just gives the thoughts the movies bring up for him, which are always very literate.

Sometimes he just writes a sentence or two about a movie.

There was a sentence about *Show Business*, an Eddie Cantor movie I hadn't thought about in decades. I used to watch it every time it was on television when I was very young, and then it stopped being on, as some movies did. I was never an Eddie Cantor fan, but there was something about this movie that I just loved.

I am probably going to get it all wrong, but here is my memory, which isn't much. It was about Eddie Cantor and Joan Somebody who I never saw in other movies, and it was a period musical about their romance and ups and downs in vaudeville and maybe they ended up on Broadway in the end. It was, of course, about show business, and while it was a small simple musical, it still made show business seem like the best place to be. Show business was about having fun and being silly and falling in love. *Show Business* gave me my path and, in my own way, I followed it.

No one ever references *Show Business*, I never read about it anywhere, or see it listed on TCM or anywhere else. It feels like the broken bunny on the shelf, something that only seems to have meaning for me.

MARCH 20

I was at a birthday party last night and someone told a story about Reese Witherspoon that didn't reflect that well on her.

Whenever I hear Reese's name, I always think about when she was shooting something in the South somewhere and her husband got pulled over for drunk driving. She was also in the car and perhaps also drunk.

"Do you know who I am?" she asked the officer.

When I read the story in the paper, I thought, yes, I now know who you are. The whole world knows who you are. You are someone who would say, "Do you know who I am?" which is not a great thing to be, in my opinion.

It's interesting to me because I think there is an essential truth there. It's that she thought she was saying one thing, but in essence, she was saying something much bigger that she was completely unaware of.

I went from person to person last night, conversation to conversation, feeling the person was telling me something that they had no idea they were telling me. I am sure I do it too because I think everyone does it. We tell each other what we want to tell each other, but have no idea we are telling each other much more than that.

Today is Sunday. So that means tomorrow is Monday. I have, of course, been thinking about the script that is out there and if anyone has read it and what their reaction is. Will I hear anything tomorrow or will it be one of the most Silent Mondays of all time?

MARCH 21

I had nightmares all night. In the last one I was working for some mysterious organization. It was like being in a 1970s conspiracy film where I didn't know if I was working for the good guys or the bad guys. I was heading back to the hotel where I was staying but then I realized that I had left all my personal belongings in the office where I was working. I went back to the office building and couldn't remember the floor or name of my employer so I had no way of getting back to the office I had been in. The security guys tried to help me, but various unpleasant people did weird things to me and to them until finally I had to just leave.

At one point much earlier in the dream, a man had suddenly thrown a big comforter over me and then got on top of me, determined to smother me. I found a small spot of air and managed to thwart his endeavor.

Then right before I reached the hotel, my things were returned to me, but I couldn't find my driver's license and starting freaking out. A group of people at the same picnic table as me tried to comfort me.

"It's just a license," one woman said.

"I know," I said. "But I hate losing things."

"What sign are you?"

"Virgo."

"Hmm," she said.

"What does 'hmm' mean?"

She wouldn't say. It seemed ominous somehow.

I was so upset about losing my license that I willed myself to wake up. Maybe this dream is like the dream in *Spellbound*, the old Alfred Hitchcock film. It could be the key that unlocks everything. Or not. It's 6:58 a.m. I don't know how I am going to get through this day. I feel like this is my day of reckoning. I can't believe day of reckonings still exist.

10:23 A.M.

This is going to be the longest day ever.

11:43 A.M.

Every inch of this house is spotless.

4:07 P.M.

Thinking a lot about the turkey farm in New Zealand today.

4:54 P.M.

Just made the sauce for a vegan cheesy broccoli rice recipe. Now going to make white bean dip. Dying.

In fact, I am moving very slowly as if I am really dying.

MARCH 22

I assume it's just going to be another day of silence. I have nothing left to clean. I am just going to wander the streets of Los Angeles.

4:13 P.M.

Okay, so it's not great. As you know, I was wandering around all day. A few hours ago, I parked my car a few blocks from my last apartment on Harper near Fountain where I lived over twenty years ago. It was the apartment with the vegetable peeler. I was walking on Sunset when my cell phone rang. It was Laura from CAA.

"Ellyn and I just wanted to give you an update," she said in a very, very cheery voice. "HBO Max read the script and loved it and want to meet."

Ellyn was late getting on, so it was just Laura and myself. "Okay," I said evenly.

Then she started to give the passes, of which there are four.

"HBO thinks they've covered the material already in *Divorce*, *Run*, and *Mrs. Fletcher*," she practically sang.

I refrained from mentioning the quality level of those programs. "Okay," I said.

"Hulu didn't feel it was their type of thing," she chirped.

"Well, *Reboot* is their thing, so fair enough," I said. That was a TV show Rob and Laura and Ellyn had really wanted me to staff on. But the script was so bad that I just couldn't.

"Amazon didn't feel it skewed young enough," she said, bouncily. "And Apple felt it was too small."

She said someone at Showtime has read it and liked it and passed it up to other people to read. Ellyn had come back by this time. "I have a call in to Amy Israel," she said.

"It's not a Showtime show," I said. "Unless they are planning to pivot after doing the exact same kind of show for three decades."

So we are now waiting to hear from Showtime, plus the four places that haven't responded yet—Netflix, Paramount+, FX, and Peacock.

So while there is definitely a chance that this show can still be bought, the odds have just dropped significantly.

My mood has not improved much, and it suddenly became nine thousand degrees out today. I was wandering Los Angeles in pants that are a little tight when it is normal, but on this very hot day, I felt as I walked around like I was in a torture chamber, sweating in my too-tight pants.

MARCH 23

I've been wandering around again today. There has been no update and I am in abject pain. I continue to move very, very slowly, as if someone hit me, or I was in a bad car accident.

After getting things at Trader Joe's, I got into my car and simply stared into space. I guess a woman wanted my spot because suddenly I felt someone looking at me. It was a woman in a car pulled up alongside me, mouthing "asshole" at me. Or more likely, now that I think about it, she was screaming it out loud, and I couldn't hear it because both of our windows were rolled up.

There is a compartment in my car that has scattered uncooked rice in it. It is in between the two front seats. It's the compartment I just throw things in and then forget what's in it. Ten years ago, I bought a stuffed animal from a neighbor named Alfie. He was a kid in Eve's preschool class, and I drive by his house many times a day. On this occasion, he had made things and was selling them, sort of like a lemonade stand but with no lemonade. I don't like to support lemonade stands for a variety of reasons, but this was a very creative endeavor that I felt I had to support.

Anyway, I bought from Alfie what I think was a rabbit that he had made with some cloth and put uncooked rice in it. And the rabbit was in the compartment for a while, but then something happened and it started leaking rice. I got rid of the rabbit, but never fully got rid of the rice.

"Why is there rice here?" Henry asked the other day. And now I am uncomfortable being a person who has been driving around in a car with uncooked rice in the front seat compartment for a decade. So I am going to go clean it now, then make a new recipe for vegan tomato soup even though it is a billion degrees today. I am going out of my mind.

4:43 P.M.

I'm not sure how well the soup turned out, but it was amazing to get rid of the uncooked rice in the car.

While I was making the soup in our tiny kitchen, it was as if I was on speed or running a marathon. I was practically sweating from the ferocity of my movements.

Then I ran to the car with a vacuum. First I cleared out all the various things I never use or would want from the compartment. I put all the pennies and other coins in a plastic bag that I have in another compartment between the front seats that isn't open. Then I vacuumed all the rice. The compartment looked like the compartment of a sane person now. It was as if this entire last few months has happened just so I would finally get the uncooked rice out of the compartment.

Oh, while I was ferociously making vegan tomato fennel soup, I received a text from Laura:

From Netflix: Hi—we like the script and want to hear where the series goes. Can we do a meeting to hear more?

And then Laura sent another text:

We're going to gather times for HBO Max and
Netflix while we have the momentum and pushing
to set at Showtime and get an answer from FX.
Peacock seems unlikely given that they are doing
the other Pete show but still following.

For those who may remember, the other Pete show had looked like it would be at Amazon I guess, but ended up at Peacock.

I wrote back:

Okay, thanks.

Then Ellyn wrote back:

Exciting.

It's not exciting. I've had meetings at Netflix where they take the meeting just to pass on the project.

When I was done racing through my tasks at home, I went to pick up Henry.

He picked up one of the fidget spinners from the rice-free compartment and started playing with it.

He'll never notice that the rice is gone, I thought to myself. Henry rarely notices things.

But a few minutes later, he looked at me, then looked at the compartment.

"Where did this rug come from?" he asked, referring to a gray cloth at the bottom of the compartment.

I smiled. "Think about it," I said.

"You bought a rug to cover the rice," he said.

"No," I said. He thought and thought but couldn't come up with anything.

Finally I had to tell him that the rug had always been there. It had just been covered up with rice and various other objects. It took a while, but ultimately Henry understood that the change was that now there was no rice.

Henry then told me he knows two people at school who've met Larry David.

"And you know me," I said. "I've met Larry David." I met him when I worked on the last season of *Seinfeld*, then would run into him socially very occasionally. And about a year or so after *Seinfeld* ended, I had a meeting with him. The special for *Curb Your Enthusiasm* had just aired, and now he was going to hire another writer to help him with the series.

The meeting was at the Broadway Deli, which now doesn't exist. It was next to Larry David's then office on the promenade in Santa Monica.

I don't remember much about the meeting except that at the end he looked at me and said, "Well I hope this hasn't been horribly painful for you."

I said, "And I hope it hasn't been horribly painful for you."

But maybe it was slightly painful for both of us, as he didn't offer me the job.

Henry looked sad as I told him the story. Clearly, he wished that I had gotten the job.

"Look," I said. "If I had gotten the job, you wouldn't exist." A few months after the meeting, I was offered a job on *Six Feet Under*, which is where I met Kate.

"It's the greatest thing in the world for me that I didn't get the job," I said. Which is a good reminder that something you think you want shouldn't necessarily be the thing you want.

I realized when I was writing Laura's text down a few minutes ago that she didn't mention Paramount. I texted her, asking if they had passed. She wrote back:

> Yes—sorry forgot to mention that. Liked the
> script but just not what they are programming

So it's not over, but the situation is pretty dire.

When I was waiting for Henry, I heard the most sooth-ing music in the car. It was a piano piece played by Simone Dinnerstein.

Composed by someone named Couperin, it is called "The Mys-terious Barricades."

It's interesting to me to think of barricades as mysterious. Barri-cades are the least mysterious things in the world. They're out there and you can't miss them. But then I thought, maybe these barri-cades are invisible. And then I started wondering what my mysteri-ous barricades are and would I ever get past them.

MARCH 24

I woke up at 4:30 a.m. from a dream where Kate was pulling my legs, and I never went back to sleep.

It is now 4:30 p.m. It has been a long silent day. No word on the HBO Max and Netflix meetings, nor anything about Showtime. It's all feeling a little like it's not going to happen.

I have been involuntarily groaning as I slow move through my day, but perhaps not as much involuntary groaning as there was yesterday.

Ginny Thomas is in the news today for her role behind the scenes on what happened on January 6. Her being the wife of a Supreme Court Justice is one of the best possible reasons I can think of for leaving this country.

5:49 P.M.

I'm literally now trudging around the house. I just trudged.

6:56 P.M.

I'm going with the flow of the universe down the toilet. Maybe I should write a *Honey, I Shrunk the Kids*, except it is about me going down the toilet. Is that what the world wants?

8:01 P.M.

I'm having a James Stewart in *It's a Wonderful Life* night. Before Clarence shows up.

MARCH 25

It's 11:23 a.m. Laura just texted:

> FX is passing—just not right for what they're looking to buy in comedy right now. Onwards!

Hmm. I wonder what onwards will look like. I texted back:

> I assumed

> It would have been an extreme pivot for them

This week could have gone a lot, lot better. I am taking Eve to a volleyball tournament in Laguna Beach this weekend. I went to Vicente Foods to get her Kind bars and, of course, got other things there but not the Kind bars, so it is a two-trips-to-Vicente day.

1:36 P.M.

I somehow just spent hours making a half-hour recipe for tempeh stir-fry for dinner tonight.

6:10 P.M.

I picked up Henry from school then went back to the kitchen to make various things. I have basically spent the whole day in the kitchen with somehow not a lot to show for it.

While I was making salad dressing, Ellyn texted:

> Amy Israel loved the pilot, the cast, everything and
> wants to meet. She's interested to hear the team
> talk about Pete in the part since the character
> is kind of the straight man. She thinks it is an
> incredible part for Glen. VERY excited.

Ever since I first met with Glenn over six months ago, Ellyn has typed "Glen" in her emails and subject headings. I have gone to great lengths, even creating new email chains with "Glenn" instead of "Glen," but it never sticks. I just have to give up.

This project doesn't seem like anything else that Showtime does, so I don't know what to think. But their apparent interest in it is a very welcome surprise.

So now it is down to HBO Max, Netflix, and Showtime, as all the other places passed. It's strange—I thought that so many of them were my safeties. None of my safeties wanted it. The Netflix meeting is set for a week from today, April 1. HBO Max has given some dates for April 12 through 14, a full two weeks from the Netflix meeting. I registered with Ellyn's assistant that this does not seem an ideal situation.

On the way home from school, Henry's Spotify account magically gave us "Just an Old-Fashioned Love Song" sung by Paul Williams. I hadn't heard or thought of the song in years. I loved the original Three Dog Night version when I was a kid and am listening to it now. When I looked it up, I saw it was written by Paul Williams, so I guess that is why he has a version of it.

I feel so lucky to have grown up with Three Dog Night and, even more to the point, to have grown up with Paul Williams. He was mainly a composer, but also he was a "personality" and would show up anywhere when I was a kid. In a movie, or on television in a crime show or a variety show or a comedy show or game show. Because his principal occupation was an off-camera one, Paul Williams didn't look like anyone else on television and had a unique presence in every way, not just visually. He was Paul Williams, like he was a duck or something, not even a person.

When I was little and he would come on whatever I was watching, I would smile and say, "There's Paul Williams" because you would never normally get someone like him on one of these shows.

Thinking about Paul Williams brings a smile to my face right now.

It was a surprise for Paul Williams to be in front of the camera, a strange and sweet and welcome surprise. I will try to keep this feeling with me, as a reminder that strange sweet surprises can happen.

MARCH 26

It's 5:30 a.m. and I am getting ready to go to the tournament in Laguna. Pray for me.

5:03 P.M.

It wasn't that bad, actually. I jumped rope on breaks and thought of ideas for future episodes of the Glenn-and-Pete show to talk about in the meetings.

I am very appreciative to have had children, because I find myself in situations I would never be in if I hadn't, such as spending eight hours in an office park in Orange County with screaming volleyball club parents. Children don't seem to ever force you to experience things like go to a tiny yet elegantly graceful museum in Paris, which is what you would love to be forced to do. They force you to go to mundane things where you have no interesting conversations, yet I am happy to have the unexpected chance to know what is out there, even if it is not interesting in any way, shape, or form.

There's a lot of oh, right, that's what's out there, when you're at a volleyball tournament in Orange County, and it's good to be forced to be exposed to it.

MARCH 27

A volleyball hit me in the head today. It didn't feel great, but I guess it could have been worse.

Volleyball club parents are constantly getting hit by volleyballs. Usually it is just your arm or your leg and you don't even take a pause in the conversation you are having with the other volleyball club parent. You keep talking as you retrieve the ball and throw it back on the court. When it hits you in the head, you have to take a pause and regroup.

The team lost all their games today. At the end of each day of the tournament, Jordan, the coach, gathers the players and has a talk about the day. Sometimes it is just five minutes.

Because they lost all their games, today's ending talk went on and on and on. All the parents (and the kids, of course) were dying to get back on the road to start their long journey in Sunday-afternoon traffic to get home. I was frustrated because not only did I want to go home, but I also honestly felt Jordan's talk would be better heard by the girls if he had it at the start of tomorrow night's club practice.

The lights went off in the gym and Jordan kept talking. After fifteen minutes, I started putting myself in his line of vision to remind him of the existence of the parents. That didn't work. Finally by some miracle he stopped talking and we got on the road to go home.

Traffic was bad. And then suddenly it got much worse. I looked at Waze, which had added a half hour to our time to get home.

Waze wanted me to get off the 405 in a mile and go a strange route around the back of LAX. Eve looked at her Google Maps or whatever it is she uses and she said there was a bad accident on the 405 near LAX.

If Jordan hadn't talked for so long, we might have been in that accident, I thought. It's a real case of the thing you want turning out to be the worst possible thing to happen to you.

Now I am home, typing this, listening to the soundtrack of *Theory of Everything*, which I go through periods of listening to over and over again. I never saw *Theory of Everything*, but one day I heard the score on the classical music station and fell in love with it. When I listen to it, I feel like I am in the opposite of the 405 in traffic. I feel like I am in a carriage on a beautiful dirt road in the English countryside, and the road is shaded by enormous trees, but occasionally you burst out of the shade and drive through lush meadows, then go back into a tree-lined area again. So that is what I am feeling, plus I am happy that everyone in this house is alive and safe.

MARCH 28

We didn't watch the Academy Awards last night, but of course we heard about Will Smith walking onstage to slap Chris Rock, and I watched the clip. I am undone. For me, this is like a MAGA rally. All the norms are going away and this society is devolving into a free-for-all. Reading various people's defense of Will Smith this morning is shocking and makes me sick to my stomach.

5:48 P.M.

I should be making notes for my pitch, but I could barely think all day, and part of the reason was the slap.

Ellyn called me around two o'clock.

"Christian called me to talk about what you would like the Netflix pitch to be like," she said.

"What did you say?" I said.

"I told him he should call you. And said you didn't like to over-rehearse what you are going to say."

"True," I said.

"He said Netflix wants a lot of details," she said.

"The last time I went to Netflix, they didn't ask for one detail," I said. But they also didn't buy the idea. So that may not be relevant, I guess.

Somehow Netflix wanting details made me not want to come up with one detail. Instead, I made a vegan carrot ginger soup and spicy shrimp tomato sauce for pasta. That took up a big part of my afternoon.

But while I was cooking, I did think of a few details and wrote them down.

Eve is back at school today. It's her birthday tomorrow. This morning, I had an idea to bring a birthday cake for her and her friends, and then see if she wanted to have dinner. The cake would come from SusieCakes, a place in Brentwood that makes the best cake in the whole entire world, I am not kidding.

Then I went to the gym and heard two trainers talking about the slap. Everyone all day everywhere has been talking about the slap. I couldn't bear to hear what the trainers were saying about the slap, so I practically ran past them to get to where I was going.

I have observed that trainers feel the need to talk at all times about all topics and offer their opinions on everything no matter what it is, as if they know anything about anything. Most of them seem to have completely different ideas about training and about nutrition, so a large portion of them have to be wrong about those areas they should be experts in.

I have never once observed a silent trainer. I don't think they make them.

When I came home, Kate and I went out to lunch with Henry, who is home on spring break.

"Are we going up to see Eve?" I asked.

"Yes," Kate said.

"What did she say?" I asked.

Kate looked confused. She had only asked someone at her boarding school if it would be okay for us to visit.

"I thought we were surprising her," she said.

"We can't surprise her," I said.

"Eve hates surprises," Henry said.

"I thought the surprise was the fun," Kate said.

"We can't surprise her," Henry and I both said.

So Kate texted Eve this:

Ok so I wanted this to be a surprise but dad
& henry said you'd hate to be surprised by: us
arriving tomorrow afternoon with a birthday cake
for you and your friends and to offer to take you
to dinner ONLY if you want that. Dinner totally
optional zero pressure!

A few minutes later, I said, "Let's guess what she will say."

"She doesn't want us to come," Henry said.

"That's what I think too," I said.

Kate said, "She will say she is happy to have us come bring a cake but she has plans for her dinner with her friends."

"No," Henry said. "She won't want us to come at all."

Kate turned to me. "And you think that too?"

"Yes, I do," I said.

The answer from Eve came on our way home from lunch:

I have a lot of things I'm doing tmrw I'm running a
girltalk meeting

Girltalk is at 6 and my sports end like
15 mins before And I have two tests on
Wednesday

"She doesn't want us to come," Henry said.

"She didn't say that," Kate said.

"She didn't say it directly, but she said it," I said.

"I don't know," Kate said.

"So you think she wants us to come?" I asked.

"I'm not sure," she said.

"I'm sure she doesn't," Henry said.

Kate turned to me. "Are you sure she doesn't want us to come?"

"Not a hundred percent," I said. "But close."

Another text from Eve came in:

I'll have susie cakes w you guys next time I'm
home

"Oh my God," Kate said. "You guys were right." Kate wrote back:

Omg, they were right!

MARCH 29

I made a lot of notes for details for Netflix this morning. Right before lunch, Christian sent:

> Could you give me a call when you have a second?
> I want to get these pitches set up so they are the
> best for you and how you like to pitch.

I called him shortly after and said I was planning to talk about the origins of the idea, then throw it to Glenn for her to talk about what she connected to in the project, then do the same with Max. I would then talk about the ideas I have for the season, and I would keep it casual and loose and would take questions from the executives as I talked.

He was good with that and asked if I wanted to have a prepitch meeting with Glenn and Max this week.

"I don't need to," I said, because I never need to have a meeting about anything. "But if they want to, I am happy to have one."

"Glenn likes to be prepared," Christian said. "She's an actress."

He texted later that Glenn did indeed want to have a meeting, so it looks like we are having one on Thursday in the morning.

I had lunch with Henry and then had a Zoom table read of a pilot for Fox that my friend Michelle wrote and directed. It was fun to visit the old network sitcom world I haven't been in for decades. Henry listened to the pilot and then, afterward, to another Zoom with other writers who gave their thoughts and pitches. The show is about two women living in Brooklyn who enter the Witness Protection Program and are forced to move to a small town.

After the Zoom, I sent in about fifteen pitches for different jokes, then played Ping-Pong with Henry.

Henry paused and looked at me at one point in the game. "Were you ever in the Witness Protection Program?" he asked. I stared at him for a while. He was genuinely asking.

"No," I finally said.

MARCH 30

I keep adding details for Netflix. The thing that is challenging about adding details is you could always add more details. That's what makes them details. It's almost infinite, maybe actually infinite. I guess it says something about living too. No matter how much you see, you can always see more.

Around 1:30 p.m., I was driving down Topanga Boulevard and my phone rang. It was an unfamiliar number and I almost didn't take it, but then decided, why not just take it?

"Hi, Bruce," a male said. I had no idea who it was. "It's Christian." Oh, right, I thought. I guess I should put his name into my phone.

"I wanted to talk about something with you. I just spoke with Ayala."

My heart sank. Ayala is Pete's agent, in case you forgot. So there's some problem with Pete, I thought. How bad is this going to be?

"Pete said he wants to commit to the entire run of the show and he wants to be in the pitches."

Christian went on to say Pete would now be in the prepitch meeting with Glenn and Max tomorrow, which might need to now change times, depending on Pete's availability.

"This is so great," I said, elated. "I can't believe this is good news. No one ever calls me with good news."

Christian almost seemed confused.

"I can call with some bad news if you want," he said.

"No, I really don't want you to," I said. "Please keep calling with good news."

Christian said he had been talking to Glenn about what she was going to say about the character in the meeting.

"She has a lot of questions for you," he said.

"Great," I said. "I may not have all the answers, but would love to have the conversation."

He mentioned something about her going granular. Sometimes that is code for something not that great, but I am choosing not to think that here.

"Of course, she likes to go granular," I said. "That is what someone of her talent and craft and intelligence does. And that's what makes her performances what they are." And that is true.

While I was talking to Christian I got a text from Kate and John:

> bruce!!!we just wrapped the special last night.
> can't wait to show it to you. and cannnnnot wait to
> get into OUR show. is there a time after the 11th
> we could all do our dinner/lunch?

I wrote back asking what was good for them. And now I am awaiting their response.

3:00 P.M.
Ellyn's assistant just emailed:

> Hi Bruce,
>
> Just got a word that Max is getting married this Friday, so
> we'll need to find a new time for the Netflix pitch . . . The
> below time works for Glenn and Max. Does it work for you
> as well?

4/8: 9am PDT

I said sure. What is confusing is that we have all known the whole time that Max is getting married this weekend. Maybe this has more to do with Pete joining the pitches. Eh, I am going to jump on the mini-trampoline in the backyard now, then maybe jump rope for a little while, then make chocolate chip blondies.

6:00 P.M.

I never heard what times Pete could do tomorrow. But since the Netflix meeting is moving to a week from Friday, and Max is getting married this weekend, I assumed my prepitch meeting with Glenn and Max for tomorrow is canceled. I just heard from Ellyn's assistant. Pete can't make it tomorrow, but Glenn and Max still want to have our meeting. Then, we can have another one with Pete next week where he can catch up. It's a lot of meetings.

The chocolate chip blondies came out very well, in my opinion.

MARCH 31

Okay, I had my meeting with Glenn, Max, and Christian this morning. I did most of the talking, telling the group about the season. I talked them through all seven episodes that come after the first script, giving them quite a lot of information.

Pitching an entire season is exhausting, like doing a short one-man show on Broadway but, of course, not getting applause or getting paid.

I genuinely liked all of their questions and thoughts, so that was nice. And they seemed to really respond to what I talked to them about. About an hour after the meeting ended, I got an email from Ellyn's assistant:

> Reaching out to set another pitch with Showtime. Are you
> good for 4/26 at 9:30am PDT? Unfortunately, it's the only
> time Showtime can currently give us.

I mean. That's about a month from now. That is really dragging this out. And now we are starting to get in a time crunch in terms of my writing the scripts. I was thinking that I could write all the episodes, but if we are aiming to start shooting in September, then ideally I would need to be done with all the first drafts by July 1. This is now becoming worrisome, but I am not going to think about it right now.

Also, Kate and John texted. We are now set for lunch on April 14. I mentioned them in the meeting, and Max said they would both be perfect for Glenn's children in the show, and I agreed.

In the afternoon, Ellyn texted:

> Bruce, Christian wrote to us after today's call,
> which he said was fantastic

I had sensed it went well, but it's always nice to hear. Christian seems very confident that more than one place will want to buy it, but as always, I remain unsure.

I put the "Theme from *Mahogany*" by Diana Ross in the show. Episode six centers all around it, and I am listening to it right now and am so happy. In the song, Diana Ross keeps asking, "Do you know where you're going to?" It's really a great question. Maybe the best one. I almost want to do this show solely so I can do an episode centered around the "Theme from *Mahogany*."

APRIL 1

Ellyn's assistant emailed this morning:

Hi Bruce,

We will now need to find a new time for HBO Max. Would some of the below work for you?

HBO MAX (all in PT):

4/19—2:30p, 3p, 4p

4/20—9:30a, 10a

4/21—12:30p

4/26—10a, 4p

Thanks!

There were too many dates and times for me to focus, so I should have just said I would do any of them.

Maybe I also couldn't focus because we are entertaining the crazy thought of relocating to New York City in the fall. Once I started talking about Pete's schedule and how this could shoot in New York in the fall, Henry and Eve started talking about relocating there. Eve has been pushing to go to school in New York, and Henry is dying to leave Los Angeles and never come back here.

"If you stay here after we go to college," he said to me a few weeks ago. "I am never coming to visit you. You can visit me."

Kate is the most reluctant to actually move, but definitely were this TV show to shoot there in the fall, she does not want to be left alone in Los Angeles for months and months, which of course we would never actually do. The truth is, for Kate and for myself, this is an opportunity for all of us to live under one roof again. It has been hard not living with Eve.

Eve keeps asking me if there is any news on the show, meaning any news on her going to school in New York. Finally I told everyone, "This is going so slowly that we have to make a decision if everyone wants to be in New York, independent of this show."

Everyone wanted New York. So Kate contacted a service that places kids in schools in New York, and she found out yesterday that there were potentially two spots available at Fieldston for Henry and Eve. She is now in Las Vegas with Eve for a tournament, and I have been filling out the Fieldston applications. I hate filling out all the data about where they went to school, where we went to school, etc. But I love writing little essays describing who Henry and Eve are, what they are interested in, and who they want to be.

We have filled out many school applications for them over the years, and I never minded writing the essays describing them. When I write about Henry and Eve, it makes me feel lucky to know them. I wonder if all parents think their children are unusual. So many kids seem so usual that it seems impossible for the parents to think they are unusual. I wish it was the kind of question I could ask someone.

"Your kid seems so ordinary," I would say.

"Yeah," the other parent might reply back. "He really is. Very, very ordinary."

Actually, I think I do know a few parents who I might have that exchange with. But I won't.

APRIL 2

Now I am on a flight to New York with Henry. We're just going for a few days for fun. Last year I supervised a pilot for Adult Swim created by Liana Finck, another *New Yorker* cartoonist. I didn't quite understand it when we first talked about it, but told her I would do it, as she needed an executive producer to get them to buy it. Then she wrote it and I fell in love with the piece, which is very autobiographical. It was funny and unique and, of course, Adult Swim passed on it. She is going to try to sell it to other places and has given me a new draft to read before I see her tomorrow morning.

Also tomorrow, I told Arturo Castro I would talk to him about a pilot he is trying to sell. He is an actor I worked with on *Mr. Corman*. He texted me last night, asking me if he could "pick my brain."

I texted back that I was traveling today, but would talk to him tomorrow.

Before takeoff this morning, Kate texted:

I was up all night in mortal fear of moving

I texted back that we didn't have to, but she said she wanted to go with the flow. I told her we could keep talking about it this week.

If my parents were alive, they would say we should make a list of the pros and cons. All their advice sounded like that, as if it had come from one article written in the 1950s, not from their own life experiences.

8:23 P.M.

Okay, what I couldn't write while I was on the plane was that I was sitting next to an extremely angry person. We were three rows from the back of the plane in very cramped seats. The man next to me was angrily texting someone for the entire length of the over five-hour flight. Henry and I were both in aisle seats across from each other. This guy was large and in the middle seat next to me, and as he angrily texted, he constantly jabbed me with his left arm and muttered what he was texting. I couldn't quite see or hear the texts.

"Blah blah blah dignity," he muttered at one point.

I asked the flight attendant for headphones and listened to classical music while reading the book I brought, which I hate.

It's a thriller you buy in an airport by Andrew Somebody, and I spent the whole flight reading it as if I didn't hate it while the man occasionally jabbed me with his angry texting.

Andrew Somebody clearly is the most heinous person, so I don't mind saying how much I hate this book. My friends Sarah and Lesley read it and I am on a text chain with them about it, so I felt I had to finish it and now I am almost done. But boy, this book is awful.

APRIL 3

I loved Liana's new draft. I wonder if the world will love it too. I hope so.

I started to get intense anxiety when I took a walk with Liana earlier and still have it hours later.

There was a James Spader movie a long time ago when James Spader was in movies, maybe it was *Bad Influence*, where his character had a disturbed brother who showed up at his door, very upset.

"I have the fear," the brother said. That's how I feel. I have the fear.

Henry and I met my friend Michael at a restaurant called Hearth in the East Village. We were early and waited for Michael outside. I looked at a flower box in front of the restaurant that had pussy willows in it.

My mother had a vase of pussy willows in our living room when I was a kid. I feel like I haven't seen or heard of pussy willows in the last forty years. I was happy to see them again.

Michael arrived just as a mad woman started walking back and forth in front of the restaurant babbling to herself, and occasionally to us. She seemed to be confused, and her hair was very disheveled.

I felt sad for her. So many people seem to be wandering around talking to themselves, living lives off the grid. She muttered something then walked into the restaurant.

Henry, Michael, and I were stunned. None of us thought she was actually going to go in the restaurant. I said we should wait a few moments before we went in, not wanting to be a part of the scene that I assumed was about to happen when they escorted her out.

But they didn't. We went in, and there she was at the bar, chatting with the friend she had obviously planned to meet there. The crazy lady wasn't crazy at all.

APRIL 4

I just jumped rope for a half hour by the Hudson River. On the way to and from the river, I passed a first-floor apartment that you can see into. On one of the walls is a painting that says: "What Are You Gonna Do."

At first I thought it is meant to remind whoever lives there, ah, what are you gonna do about that thing that bothers you? Just accept whatever it is and don't think about it.

But then I thought, maybe it is genuinely asking the question: What are you gonna do? By that I mean, it is telling the person to stop thinking about whatever they might want to do. It is time to just do it, as Nike used to say and may still say. In either case, I guess I am wondering, What am I gonna do?

My phone call for Arturo to "pick my brain" got pushed to today. He said he sold his show to Amazon about a group of immigrant friends, but now they wanted him to come up with a hook.

"So I wanted to talk to you," he said. "Not that I expect you to give me a hook." But it felt somehow like perhaps he did.

He described the character he would play as someone who feels everyone else has grown up but he hasn't. He mentioned that he hears his ex-girlfriend is having a baby.

"Maybe he and his friends inherit a baby," I said. "That's a hook. It's the hook they used in *Three Men and a Baby*."

"Great," he said, and we hung up seconds later. It was about a seven-minute call.

"I also really wanted to connect with you," he said at the end.

"Oh, right," I said. "Sure."

I wonder if Amazon will go for it. I would never watch that show in a million years, so I am assuming they will.

Yesterday, Kate got hit in the face with a volleyball at Eve's tournament. Unlike when I got hit in the head last weekend, Kate has a concussion and feels terrible. I just talked to her while she is lying in the hotel room, resting.

"I asked Joe what happened," she said, referring to one of the other parents. "I have no memory of it."

"I wondered if you knew," he said. He then told her that a ball was going to go out, but Eve went for it, not realizing it was going to go out, and she was the one who slammed it into Kate's face.

Kate laughed. "It's perfect," she said.

Oh, one more thing. While I was jumping rope, someone my age walked by me and I thought, I wonder if that was my neighbor that moved away when I was five or six.

Ever since someone from college didn't recognize me at my friend Willie's funeral in the fall (and I didn't recognize him), I know the old me looks nothing like the young me. So now I keep seeing people and wondering if they are the older versions of people I knew years ago.

Yesterday, a crazy-looking old man walked into the Strand bookstore, and I thought: That might be the old version of the first producer I worked for when I was twenty-one.

Now that I know that anyone can turn into someone totally

different, part of me thinks I am constantly walking by old versions of people I used to know and not even having any awareness of it.

APRIL 5

It's five o'clock and we're on a plane back to Los Angeles about to take off. It's not a very glamorous group of people on this plane, and that is all I will say about that.

Ellyn's assistant tentatively set a prepitch meeting earlier today with Pete, Glenn, Max, and Christian, but then it never happened because I believe Pete couldn't make it. Now she is trying to set another time on Wednesday or Thursday before our meeting at Netflix on Friday.

I'm having one of those days where I check to make sure I have my phone, my wallet, and my reading glasses constantly. I would say it was because I am traveling, but it has been like that ever since I woke up.

At one point an hour ago, I was very agitated in the airport when one of our boarding passes ripped into two pieces.

"What does it matter?" Henry asked.

"I don't know," I said. I thought for a second. "I'm sorry. I'm having a—— day," naming a person we know who is always very agitated.

"That's okay," he said.

"No, I know it's not fun to be around. I don't know why I've turned into——."

"It's your choice to be——."

"No," I said. "It's not."

Somehow now I am calmer. I used our miles to get better seats on the way back. We are sitting in a side row of two seats next to each other. Henry is ecstatic we have so much room, and I am ecstatic that no one will be assaulting me as he angrily texts and mutters.

Henry just now looked over at me typing this.

"You're on page a hundred eighteen!?" he said in disbelief. He knows about my journal, and for some reason it has really captured his imagination.

"I know," I said. "When I started writing, I thought, I guess I will know if someone is going to buy this Glenn project by page fifty."

He laughed.

"And then," I said, "I thought I would know by page seventy-five. And then I was really sure I would know by somewhere in the nineties, positive that it would happen before page one hundred."

Henry laughed again.

"Now I don't have any page number I think I will know by," I said, which is really true.

Sometimes I sing made-up songs in my head, or out loud when I am alone. I just went to the airplane bathroom and out popped the one that is in my head right now.

"Zitty little kitties," I sang out. "Why are kitties zitty? They're zitty because they're kitties!"

I feel like this one is going to be stuck in my head for days. Some stay, some don't, but this feels like one that will stay.

APRIL 6

I went to the gym and was horrified by the images from Ukraine that were on CNN. How is this all going to end?

The meeting with Pete and everyone else is set for tomorrow afternoon at 2:30 p.m.

As I type this, Kate is lying on the couch, trying to recover from her concussion. When you can't look at screens, you are a true invalid.

COVID numbers are rising this week due to the Omicron variant. It feels like this is permanent.

I had a bad night's sleep, so perhaps it is too much to ask of me to make any of this interesting, but I wanted to keep everyone up-to-date.

Earlier today I went to Vicente Foods, then as I was leaving remembered that I hadn't gotten what I had gone there for—sauerkraut. I turned around and got it. I would have killed myself if I had had to drive back for the sauerkraut.

APRIL 7

This is the second day of my being driven mad by step four of the Fieldston application. It should be a simple thing, as all it is asking for is the registrar's name and email address. But no matter what I do, it won't let me put it in. I have tried over a dozen times and have sadly called and emailed Fieldston for help. They called me back at 4:00 a.m. when I was asleep.

3:36 P.M.
Kate told me I was the problem, not step four. I was expecting to get a green check mark when I finished what I was supposed to do.

The green check mark only comes after they get the paperwork that step four allows them to get. She usually is in charge of the grades/report cards areas of applications, but since she is concussed, it is my first time.

It was actually a profound moment for me, a reminder that the real problem is never step four or whatever I am having trouble with, it is always me. Obviously, it is something I need to relearn every five seconds.

The Pete meeting was at two thirty. Christian, Max, and I were there on time. We chatted for a while. And then chatted for a while more.

Christian started texting Glenn.

"I wonder where Glenn and Pete are," he said.

"Maybe they're having their own Zoom," I said.

Finally Glenn came and we chatted some more. Christian texted with Ayala, I think, or maybe someone in her office.

"Pete's sick," he said around three or so. We talked about various things, then Christian ended by asking us all a question.

"How do you feel about pitching to Roku?" he said. "Roku is very interested in hearing the pitch. They are asking about when it would shoot and about the budgets."

The group all talked about how Roku's need for programming would probably mean they would make an offer, which would help it become a competitive situation with the other platforms. So we all agreed to pitch to Roku.

When this happened, I felt a huge sense of relief float through my body. They all talked about Roku making it a competitive situation with someone else. But my feeling was Roku needs this and the other three don't. So Roku seems like a very good safety. In other words, it made me feel that this now is much closer to definitely happening than when we were pitching to just the other three.

So now I am going to iron five shirts, jump for twenty minutes in the backyard, then make the half-hour tempeh stir-fry that takes hours.

5:10 P.M.

Tomorrow's pitch has been changed from 9:00 a.m. to 8:30 a.m. because Netflix had a conflict. As I prepared the stir-fry, the most wonderful music came on the classical radio station. It's called "Happiness Does Not Wait" by Ólafur Arnalds. I was suddenly filled with a wave of inner peace, so indeed happiness did not wait, at least not today.

APRIL 8

At 6:39 last night, I got a text from Max with a screenshot of a text chain between him and Pete and then a text:

> Pete texted apologies and I filled him in Did I miss
> anything?

I gave him a few little things to tell Pete about the pitch—how long he should speak, etc.

Then at 7:47, I got a text from Rob at CAA, who is back from paternity leave:

> Bruce, we're just making sure the i's are dotted
> for the pitch tomorrow! We're excited!!! As a
> heads-up, Pete's agent was concerned tomorrow's
> time might be too early for hm and asked to see
> if we could push the pitch, which we cannot bc of
> everyone's schedules and we don't want to lose
> this time where we end up having to wait another
> month (when we know the same thing could just
> as easily happen then)

> She said he'd be there and asked if the group
> had any notes from today to pass along to him. I
> assume the answer is no, but let us know if you do

> I think we should all brace for the potential that he
> shows up late or that he's a no show. Not worried
> in either scenario since you guys have this down
> but just think we should be prepared!

I texted Rob, Laura, and Ellyn that Max and I had been texting and that Pete was definitely planning to be in the pitch.

Ellyn left me a voice message shortly thereafter. While Pete had been sick at 2:30 p.m., he was now going out to a premiere and was expecting to have a late night. Since he is doing *SNL*, I assumed he is on the East Coast.

"That would be eleven thirty for him," I said to Henry and Kate at dinner. "That's a late night." We all took guesses at what time he was planning to go to bed. I assumed it would be around 4:00 a.m.

I woke up this morning, dreading having to pitch. Shortly after I woke up, I saw an item about Pete on Twitter. He had been holding hands with Kim Kardashian at the premiere of her new reality show. The premiere was in Los Angeles.

Uh-oh, I thought. Now I understood why 8:30 a.m. was too early. It didn't seem likely he would show.

When I get nervous, I sweat profusely. By 8:25 a.m., my shirt was drenched and smelled terrible. I put on a new shirt and paced for a few minutes.

At 8:28, I clicked on the Zoom link. It told me my Zoom data or whatever it is was out-of-date and I needed to reinstall Zoom.

This can't be happening, I thought. I was just on a Zoom yesterday. So I started to try and install Zoom. I am sure I made mistakes because it took me several tries.

By 8:31, I did it successfully. The host hadn't shown up yet. And then the host did. Reader, Pete was on the Zoom. Christian was the one who didn't show. He was supposed to be the emcee.

A man from Netflix in the upper-left-hand corner box said, "Should we all begin?"

I said, "Christian isn't here yet. I don't want to be unkind."

He said, "Well, we're here" in a way that told me I should start talking, and so I did.

There were about five or six Netflix executives. I told them about why I wrote the script and what I wanted to do with the show. Then I handed it over to Max, who spoke for a few minutes.

I think Christian showed up in the Zoom around then—he was in his car, clearly racing to wherever he really wanted to be when he was in the Zoom. I felt bad for him. I would have been miserable in that situation. I am always early for things, even things I don't want to go to at all.

Max handed it over to Pete, who talked for a while, then he and Glenn talked together for a while, then Glenn talked for a while.

Max, Pete, and Glenn were all impressive. I was having the best time not talking and was dreading pitching all the episodes of the season that hadn't been written yet, which was what would happen when Glenn was done.

But eventually I had to and even though there seemed to be somewhat tepid responses to what hopefully were funny moments in the episodes, it all seemed to go very well.

After I was done talking, each Netflix person had questions or thoughts and all of them seemed very engaged and understood the goals of the show.

This is going surprisingly well, I thought to myself. It felt like they really might buy it.

Then mercifully, at 9:20, Glenn exclaimed, "I'm late. I have to catch a plane and I still have packing to do." And magically, the meeting was over.

Very shortly after, I talked to Christian. I explained that I hadn't wanted to start the meeting without him. He then said he had already spoken to someone at Netflix. They loved the pitch but had been "burned" by some other comedy shows they had bought from a pitch, so they were asking to see a script for a second episode, which I would be paid to write.

Huh, I thought. I was not expecting this, as I have never heard of this step happening.

"It's very positive," Christian said. "They really love everything everyone said. They just want to know what will keep the audience watching."

We talked for a while and the dreaded word "propulsive" was used.

"This show is never going to be propulsive," I said sadly at one point. But I left the conversation thinking, at least the pitch was received positively, and I learned some things to do differently in the subsequent pitches. Since HBO Max is still the goal, I felt okay about everything.

It is now the end of the day, and I am exhausted. In fact, I have spent the whole day being exhausted, ever since 9:20 a.m.

I just got this email from Ellyn's assistant:

> Hi Bruce,
>
> Max's assistant just let us know Max is no longer able to make Showtime on 4/26 @ 9:30a work anymore. The only other avail they have that week is 4/27 @12p PT, unless we want to push to May.
>
> Let me know if you're good to reset for then! Thanks

This experience just keeps getting longer and longer.

APRIL 9

I started making notes for the second episode. It's sort of relaxing but at the same time nerve-racking.

APRIL 10

I made more notes for the second episode. In the late afternoon, I was jumping rope in front of the house when I saw a car pull up in front of the house next door where an older couple, Matt and Debbie, live. Then some little kids poured out of the back seat. Matt and Debbie have two sons. and this was clearly one of them and his family. When I moved into this house, their two sons were teenagers, basically the same ages as Henry and Eve now. Once, Matt and Debbie went away, and their sons had a big party.

Our bedroom is close to their backyard, and Kate and I couldn't sleep because it seemed like there were over a hundred teenagers over there. And now that I think of it, maybe there were. I was mad at the time, but now I have nostalgic feeling for the loud teenage party next door.

An hour later, Kate and I took a walk before dinner. We ran into Chris, another neighbor. He mentioned he said good-bye to Anne and John, the couple who live in the house on the other side of our house.

"It was weird," Chris said. "Because it was the final good-bye."

He explained that they were going to live in a cottage next to one of their sons' houses up north. I had known that was the plan for when things became too hard for Anne and John.

John and Anne are in their eighties, and he has a degenerative illness, which has made this past year very difficult for him.

"He's barely able to walk anymore," Chris said. "He doesn't have any balance. And you know how he used to love to walk."

I nodded. Every day of the first year of the pandemic, I would see him out walking in the morning, always wearing his extremely big hat.

"A couple of months ago, we had to go over there and help them because he fell down," I said.

"So did we," Chris said, referring to his wife, Elaine.

"He was really hurt," I said. "We had to wait for the paramedics."

"We waited for the paramedics too," Chris said. Then he added, "You really see the cycle of life in this neighborhood."

APRIL 11

I made more notes on the outline for the second episode, then worked on getting all the items Fieldston needs for Henry's and Eve's applications. I felt bad for Anne and John, so I made them chocolate chip cookies. It's sort of the opposite of a welcome to the neighborhood gesture. But then I couldn't bring myself to walk over to their house to give the cookies to them, so I didn't. Maybe I can tomorrow.

After I picked up Henry from school, I dropped him off at home, then drove up to Santa Barbara because Eve needed a ride to volleyball club practice. That's where I am now, sitting in the stands far away from everyone, because everyone who didn't have COVID in December and January is getting it now from the new variant. My friend Natalie texted me this earlier:

Also think I have covid but all tests neg so dyin
dyin

I talked to her on the ride up. She described her symptoms, and it definitely sounds like she has it.

After I hung up with her, I listened to Ezra Klein interview Fiona Hill about the situation in Ukraine. She was not at all hopeful and there was a lot of talk about the dark times ahead. I turned it off four minutes before it actually ended, because I couldn't hear the word "famine" anymore.

I keep wondering why I never heard of anyone visiting Ukraine when people traveled to Europe back when people traveled. What kept everyone from going to Ukraine?

APRIL 12

I was supposed to have lunch with Kate and John on Thursday, but got this text from Kate this morning:

> BRUCE john herniated the disc he just has surgery
> on, he's in hellish pain and was in the ER. Let's
> make this lunch a call, though it's unclear if he can
> even manage that by Thursday.
>
> Will get right back to you

I texted back:

> That's terrible

> I can do it whenever no urgency

She wrote back:

> Ya he's really in hell

But then didn't hear if we are indeed having a call on Thursday. It seems unlikely.

I took my Kate to the concussion doctor today, and he said she was okay to do most things now. I thought I was going to have to drive her around all day, but now that she can drive, I had the afternoon free. I just started writing the second script, even though I wasn't planning to. It was like my brain really needed to get it out of me.

APRIL 13

I was in a daze all day, writing. Periodically I would get intense waves of anxiety, but I strangely kept being able to write. After I picked up Henry, I experienced a particularly large wave of anxiety while being stuck in traffic and made some sort of noise.

"What's wrong?" he said.

I explained, and said I felt bad that he had to have such an anxious person for a parent.

When we got home, I read an article in the *New York Times* about David Mamet. He has a new book and has been doing interviews and keeps talking about how the last president did a great job, which is extremely creepy. I never liked David Mamet before, but now I find him truly disturbing.

Oh, and Natalie tested positive finally.

APRIL 14

I had another dazed writing day. I am about four pages away from finishing my rough draft. At one point during the day, I thought, this is garbage. But now I love it. Of course, I haven't reread what I wrote. It really could be garbage. But hopefully, it's not.

My friend Sarah's wedding is in exactly one month. We had to RSVP today, on the last day. I have been putting it off because I was hoping Eve would come. She has a volleyball tournament, but I kept praying it would be canceled.

When I RSVPed, I got anxious. Maybe it was because Sarah asked me to read something during the ceremony. I have been filled with anxiety about what I would read. Every time I think about finding the perfect thing to read, I get filled with such anxiety that I can't do it.

"You have to talk to her," Kate said. I have also been thinking that maybe I am just not strong enough to talk at her wedding, just like I wasn't strong enough to talk at Willie's memorial.

"You've seen me talk on millions of panels in front of hundreds of people," I said to Kate. "What is happening to me?"

"I don't know," she said. "But you might have to tell her what's happening."

I texted Sarah to ask her to talk on my drive to pick up Henry. She texted back:

Yes—I'll be walking in like 5 mins

When we talked, I just couldn't tell her about my anxiety and fears of speaking at her wedding. I love her too much. And then magically, as we were talking about Eve and her volleyball team, I realized I would write down what we were talking about and it would then be the perfect thing to read at her wedding, and the anxiety subsided. We hung up when I had to urinate at the park next to Henry's school.

I picked up Henry, and on the way home, Spotify was telling him to listen to a song by the Monkees. I was overjoyed. And then we played more Monkees songs on the way home. It was so soothing. Their TV show, *The Monkees*, was such a unique and interesting thing to watch when I was a kid. *The Monkees* had a real singular feeling to it, which so many, in fact most, television shows don't have. There is nothing more soothing to me than watching something and hearing a distinctive voice that makes it unlike any other voice in the world. Plus, *The Monkees* had a real visual style that compelled you to keep watching it, even when it made no sense whatsoever.

I ran into Vicente Foods to get all the ingredients to make spicy shrimp pasta. Then went home and thought, I wonder how much Parmesan cheese we have. We had exactly a third of a container, which is basically how much Henry uses on one portion of pasta.

So it was a two-Vicente-trips day, but not really, because I hadn't needed what I had forgotten.

APRIL 15

Okay, I finished the first draft of the second script today. I don't know what to think or who to tell. I am exhausted, so I will sit on it for a moment before deciding what to do with it.

Sometimes when I am writing a script, it is like I am having a long dream where I am on the most relaxing vacation with the most interesting people. Then, when I am finished writing, it is like I woke up and am in reality again, where everything is scary and it feels like there is no hope.

Also, someone died in our driveway last night. When I went out to take Henry to school this morning, I saw that the driveway was covered in feathers. Some were strangely affixed to the cement—I'm not sure what exactly happened or to whom, but it definitely looks like murder.

APRIL 16

Henry is in his room with the door closed, listening to "Strawberry Fields Forever." It's like it's 1973 in this house and he is dropping acid.

I was jumping on the mini-trampoline around eight this morning, and heard sounds from next door.

John and Anne are getting ready to go, I thought. I should go over there and bring the cookies.

All week I couldn't bring myself to bring the cookies to John and Anne. I just wasn't able to face this good-bye. Two days ago, I put the cookies in the freezer so they wouldn't be stale when I was able to face the good-bye.

I kept bouncing for a while, then talked to Kate. But I still didn't go over.

Then, I happened to be passing the front door and through the window I saw the shadow of a person approaching the front door. I could tell by the shadow it was Anne. I opened the door, and we both started talking at the same time.

"I was going to bring you cookies today," I said as she said something about wanting to say good-bye to us because they were leaving.

"I didn't know you knew," she said.

"Chris told us a few days ago," I said, but she seemed not to hear me.

Kate came to the front door as I went into the kitchen and maniacally started putting cookies from the freezer into a smaller bag for her.

Then I gave Anne the cookies. I could tell Kate thought the visit was over, but I knew it was just beginning. Anne had come to bring us back to her house to say good-bye to John, who can't really walk anymore.

On the way over, I said to Anne, "I can't imagine what this is like for you. What is it like for you?"

"Horrible," she said. She explained that they had lived in their house for fifty-two years and now that they were moving up north they had to get rid of almost all their things. And also, they had to deal with all the logistics of renting their house out.

"I haven't changed our bank accounts yet," she said, clearly overwhelmed by her situation.

"Well, that can wait," I said.

We reached her house and John was at the kitchen table, clearly not doing well at all. Their son and daughter-in-law were around, helping them out, before driving them to their house tomorrow.

I talked to John briefly, and he put out his fist, to fist-bump me, so I fist-bumped him. Then Anne wanted us to take something, whatever I wanted, from the house. It wasn't clear what they were taking to the cottage, so I didn't want to take something they wanted. I didn't want to take anything at all, but it felt like I had to take something, as if to say, I will remember you.

"Do you want a bird picture?" she said. They had many big photographs of birds that I assume one of them had taken. I definitely didn't want a bird picture.

"We can't take a bird picture," I think Kate said, implying that they really should hold on to their bird pictures.

I saw a tiny mirror it seemed no one would bring anywhere for any purpose.

"I'll take this mirror," I said. Then Anne kept showing us into other rooms, clearly wanting me to take something else. Or maybe she just wanted to keep looking at all her things before they went away and she never saw them again. We reached a hall filled with more big photographs of birds.

"Do you want a bird picture?" she asked again.

"No," I said. Next to the big photographs of birds were about ten pen-and-ink drawings of buildings.

"John drew those," Anne said. "Now he can't use his hands."

We went into a different hall that had a shelf filled with children's picture books.

"I suppose your children are too old for these," she said.

"Yes," Kate and I both said. My eyes landed on the original edition of *Chitty Chitty Bang Bang*, which I had owned as a child.

"I'll take *Chitty Chitty Bang Bang,*" I said and told her how much I loved the illustrations by John Birmingham.

We then went back to the kitchen and said good-bye to John, and their son and daughter-in-law.

"We took a mirror," I said. "So we will think of you whenever we look at ourselves." At least I think that is what I said. Or maybe Kate and I both said versions of it. Then we stumbled back to our house, shaken.

It was a disturbing encounter. There was so much sadness and pain in the interaction. They are both facing not only the end of their life here of more than fifty years, but also of John's life and, of course, Anne's too. I mean, anyone who goes into that house in that moment is facing the end of their lives too. It just may not be as immediate.

When Grandma Rose, my father's mother, died, she was ready to go. She was in her nineties and was tired of her life on earth.

"I'm done," she said, and clearly she was. I didn't get that feeling from John and Anne today. I felt the pain of wanting to go on with life as it was, not as it was going to be, and it is truly unbearable.

This had a real "I don't want to go" energy, in every sense of the word.

It is now four thirty, hours later, and I am still disoriented and not thinking properly. I am in the kitchen, desperately trying to think of something to make but having no idea what it should be.

Maybe I will just make white bean dip because it is easy and I won't have to think in any way.

5:54 P.M.

The parsley I needed for the white bean dip had gone bad, so I didn't make anything. Just now, I took the recycling out, and even though I swept up tons of feathers yesterday, there were still remains of the bird murder lying on the doormat.

APRIL 17

I sent the script for the second episode to Ellyn, Rob, and Laura this morning. Then frenetically made carrot ginger soup, chocolate-covered sugar cookies, and vegan cheesy broccoli rice for dinner.

A feather from the bird murder showed up in the living room, seemingly brought into the house by Henry's flip-flop shoe.

APRIL 18

Okay, Ellyn and Laura read the script and were very positive. So I sent it to Glenn, Pete, Max, and Christian. I'm nervous!!

I got a text from Kate Berlant this morning:

John is talking to a surgeon today, it looks
like he's going to have to go back under the
knife (he had surgery already just a few months
ago) We are currently editing the sketch special
& there is a sketch in there which feels close to
the personas we want to develop for our show—as
soon as we can, we'll send to you! Peacock has
been really great to work with & we are hoping if
they like our special they would be receptive to a
series!

It ended with a prayer emoji. I wrote back:

Re John that is terrible
Re all else great!!

Maybe in the end, I will just end up supervising them at Peacock. It is not how I saw my year going, but it could be fun, I guess, I hope, probably not.

APRIL 19

Liana sent a copy of the latest draft of her pilot to her agent at the end of day yesterday and cc'd me. I then forwarded the script to Ellyn, Rob, and Laura because they all wanted to see it. It's so beautiful and hilarious and unique that I am sure no one will want it.

APRIL 20

Yesterday was a really bad day. I never heard anything about the script for the second episode from Glenn, Max, or Christian. Also, the HBO Max meeting was never reconfirmed for the following morning. So I had a bad feeling all day long. Then around six, as I was making dinner, I got a phone call from Ellyn and Rob. They informed me that Glenn was canceling the HBO Max meeting that was supposed to be today because she was "spooked" by the second script. Apparently, she has many problems with it, and Max also has "notes" and while Christian tried to get her to move forward with the HBO Max meeting, she didn't want to. Ellyn said Christian said she was "crabby" because she has just gotten home from a trip.

There was talk of Glenn, Christian, Max, and myself all meeting at 10:00 a.m., the time the HBO Max meeting was supposed to happen, but no one sent me a link, so I am not sure that is going to happen.

11:01 AM

I got sent a link for the Zoom a little after nine. I was dreading the meeting and bounced on the mini-trampoline for a while, then went to shave at ten of ten. Christian called just as I was finishing shaving.

"Glenn reread the script and now likes many things about it," he said. "We agreed that she should put her thoughts on paper instead of having the Zoom. She's gone to the dentist."

"So is the HBO Max meeting going to be rescheduled?" I asked.

"Yes," he said. "After she gets her thoughts down on paper. She needs to be able to talk about the character eloquently in the pitch."

I reminded him she talked eloquently about her character in the pitch at Netflix.

"Well, now that she read the second script, she needs to figure out what she is now going to say," he said.

I didn't understand, but said I understood.

I then had the Zoom just with Max. He was very positive about the episode and just had one note, which was to see more of Glenn and Pete alone in the first half of the script.

I mentioned we never heard when we were going to pitch to Roku.

"I just read some article about Roku and I think they died," he said. He then talked about their business model and how there was some flaw in it that made them not able to afford to do programming.

My friend Sarah has a meeting on the books with Roku that got set yesterday, but I didn't mention that to Max. He's probably right that Roku has died, which is very bad for us.

Even though things have turned around since last night, I still have sort of a bad feeling about everyone. Except for Pete, of course. Both before I spoke to Christian and Max, and after, I have been wandering around the house, leaving my reading glasses some- where, then not being able to find them, then finding them, then losing them again. It is like I have been hit by a car and am in shock.

5:07 P.M.

Yesterday, I was telling my friend Rachel a story about my grand-mother and my father. It was that every single time we arrived home after an airplane flight, my father would race to the telephone to tell his mother that we were alive. Once, for some reason, he wasn't quick enough. The telephone rang.

"Why didn't you call me?" Grandma Rose asked, very upset.

"So she controlled your father?" Rachel asked, but it was more of statement. I am not sure though whether she actually controlled him or just controlled his behavior after airplane flights.

"Did she flee another country to live in the United States?" Rachel asked. "That can cause a lot of fear."

"No, she was raised here," I said. Rachel looked confused, as if that meant she shouldn't have been so fearful.

"Where are your ancestors from?" she said.

"I don't know," I said. "Eastern Europe?"

"You don't know where you are from?" she said in disbelief. She looked at me as if I was out of my mind.

"I think my mother's parents were from Germany," I said. "And maybe my father's grandparents came from Russia. I think."

But none of that sounded quite right. Later, I texted my broth-ers to see if they knew where we were from.

Andrew wrote back that he didn't know where my father was from. This is what he wrote about my mother's parents:

I think that Abe was from Odessa, in the Ukraine,
and that Fannie was from Poland.

Mike wrote this about my father's mother:

I think Rose's parents were from Austria.

And this is what he wrote about my mom's parents:

I thought Abe & Fanny met in the Old Country.

Which made Andrew write back:

Maybe I'm wrong

I don't even know what the Old Country is, but am choosing not to ask. He suggested I ask my Uncle Martin, so I emailed him. I also emailed my cousin George, who was really my father's cousin, asking where his parents were from. George wrote back:

> We are talking about your great-grandparents Abraham & Leah Cohen Kaplan; Moe (Morris) Kaplan's parents' Abraham, who I knew as Zayde, was born in Vilna around 1860 and came to the USA around 1880. His father's name was Moses.

> Leah was the daughter of Wolfe and Zelda Cohen and was born in the USA—New York City?

I had to look up what Vilna is or was. It's the capital of Lithuania. Odessa, Lithuania, the Old Country—it still seems all the same to me. It's strange that none of this really means anything to me. Or obviously to my brothers. But we must be in the minority, since it seems a lot of people care about where they are from. I wish someone could tell me why.

    6:01 P.M.

I just got off the phone with my friend Gary. I told him about the last twenty-four hours.

"Why did you do that?" he said, about giving the script to the group.

"I thought they would be excited to see all their ideas synthesized into an episode," I said. "I thought my agents and manager were telling me to give it to them."

"Well, I never would have told you to give it to them," he said.

"I don't even care if this happens anyway," I said. "If it doesn't happen, it's just one step in my life. Everything leads to something else," I said.

"Does it?" he said.

"Yes," I said. "So no matter what happens, it will be okay. Even if this leads to nothing. I would like nothing. Right now, nothing seems preferable to this."

"Definitely," he agreed.

APRIL 21

This used to be my father's birthday. If he were alive, he would be ninety-five. It is strange to think that both he and my mother could still exist, as both seem so far from being able to exist.

My father looms so large in my head, even larger now than he did when he was alive. That seems one of the worst parts of fatherhood. I don't want to loom large in anyone's head.

He loved movies, especially musicals. We went to see *That's Entertainment* when it opened in 1974. It was a tribute to the MGM musicals of the 1930s, 1940s, and 1950s, but mostly the 1940s. That summer, because of *That's Entertainment*, I think, Channel 5 showed a classic MGM musical every Saturday night at 11:30.

My father was really psyched, although I don't think we used that word back then. He got either Yodels or Ring Dings for us, and we stayed up much later than we ordinarily did to watch the films each week. Most were classics like *Easter Parade* or *On the Town*, but there were also weird ones like *Two Sisters from Boston*. I remember watching *The Barkleys of Broadway*, a later Astaire and Rogers movie that no one ever seemed to reference, but I liked it. Ginger Rogers is one of those actresses that has a real truth to her. When she was upset, she really seemed upset. And when she was happy, she genuinely seemed happy. It's strange that more actors don't have that quality.

Around that time, someone asked me what I wanted to do when I grew up and I said, "Be a tap dancer." I feel like that ended by the time that summer ended, but after these last two days, I really wish I were a tap dancer. Maybe in a way I am. When I worked for Carol Matthau, she used to say, "We're all just tap dancers," and now I really understand it in a way I hadn't then.

I don't know what to do with myself while I am waiting for Glenn to put her thoughts on paper, so I am making a new recipe for a creamy white bean soup with kale for dinner right now, even though it is before noon.

6:00 P.M.

I got this email from my uncle Martin today:

> My mother, your maternal grandmother, was born and grew up in Bialystok. I don't know where her mother was born but it was probably in Bialystok or vicinity. Bialystok was in the "pale" of the western part of the tzarist Russian empire where Jews were confined to live. At that time and now, it is in Poland.

I know very little about my father's family. He was born and lived in Odessa, which was also in tzarist Russia at that time and is now part of Ukraine.

Also, I got a document from Glenn where she explained who the character I wrote is. It seems wildly in opposition to every line of dialogue. It was also very rude in reference to my writing. It was an unkind page overall.

I assumed everything was over. Then I spoke to Ellyn and Laura, who said I should call Christian. I called him, and he says everything is great. He said I should hop on the phone with Glenn tomorrow and maybe ask Max, who has been talking to Glenn, to also be on the call. So I did ask Max, and he says everything is great.

"I'll be in a mix all day tomorrow so I'm not available," he said.

"That's fine," I said. "But I would like to get your thoughts now on the document. You don't think the character she is talking about is in opposition to the character as written?" I asked.

"No," he said.

"And you don't think the tone is completely different than the tone of the two scripts?" I asked.

"I think you should just talk to her," he said.

"Okay," I said, so I assume Christian's office will facilitate that. When I think of Glenn, I am filled with hate but am trying not to succumb to it.

7:24 P.M.

I tried to schedule a call with Glenn with Christian's office. His assistant Chloe wrote back that since Christian and Max wouldn't be able to be on the call, they would prefer that the four of us all speak Monday.

APRIL 22

I had an incredible day. Maybe I needed to have this week in order to have this day. It is Earth Day, and some people are being silent.

Henry told me it has something to do with gay rights, but on the internet it says it has to do with *Silent Spring*, a book I've always heard of but have no idea what it is and have never wanted to find out. In any case, I decided to be silent after I dropped Henry off at school and then be silent all day long until I picked him up at 3:30 p.m. So it would be a shortened version of all day long.

I went to the gym, then instead of going home, I decided to go to the sculpture garden at UCLA, one of my favorite places in Los Angeles. It has been in my mind to go there for some reason and today I found out why. I parked my car off campus and entered at the bottom of UCLA and walked upward. I know in a general way where the sculpture garden is, but I always make wrong turns on my way to finding it. UCLA became like a beautiful maze as I slowly made my way to it, and then finally, there it was. And I was filled with the most intense feeling.

All throughout the last few months, I have said over and over in my meetings about this script that it came to me at a time where I was very upset about the pain and sadness and brutality and horrors of today's world post 2016. I wanted to write a script as a form of activism. Initially I thought it would be calling out hypocrites and immorality and unethical politicians. As I started to make notes for that idea, I was filled with hate for the world. And then I realized I was doing the exact opposite of what I should do. I wanted to write a show that reminds us that while all these ugly things feel like our reality today, there are other things that are just as real, even if we can't see them or feel them in this moment—hope, beauty, faith, art, and love. Those are just as real. I know I just said it, but I am saying it again.

As I told this over and over to Glenn, then Glenn and Max, then Glenn and Max and Pete, then Netflix, I never actually felt it. It was just words. Today, in the sculpture garden I felt it.

I started beaming while I was in the garden. I had a giddy expression like a child. And I felt the air on my face for what seems like the first time in a hundred years. I heard the sounds of the wind in the trees. And I felt myself breathing, as if I hadn't really taken a breath before.

It's not just that I love the sculptures in the garden. I love how they are placed in their environment. And I love all the sleek mid-century buildings surrounding the garden. And somehow I love the people who are in the garden, without knowing them in any way.

I left the garden and made my way back down to my car. I passed the UCLA students and felt all their hope and passion and excitement about their lives. I felt their sense of possibility. It felt amazing.

At one point I heard a loud group of people. Usually, I have auditory sensitivity, where almost anything hurts my ears, but in this moment all I heard was a beautiful cacophony, as if all of us were indeed beautiful no matter what we sounded like.

I turned a corner and entered a courtyard and saw the people and felt an intense wave of love for them. I continued walking down toward my car in a rapturous state. I felt like I had the most wonderful secret in the world without even knowing what the secret was. I assume everyone I smiled widely at thought I was an insane person.

On my way down, I encountered the UCLA botanical garden, which must have existed my entire time in Los Angeles, but no one I know has ever referenced it, and I have certainly never been in it or known it existed. I walked through the botanical garden, at one with the world. And just before I exited to the street, which was a block from my car, I saw two people working in the garden, and I thought, they have the best job in the whole world. In that moment if they had turned to me and said, "Do you want to come work with us?" I would have said immediately, "Yes, I do."

Maybe I really should be a UCLA botanical garden worker, I thought. I am not sure what you need to do to qualify for that job. And they obviously have some people who do it currently and I don't know if they are hiring, or will be hiring in the future. But in the moment, it seemed like the perfect occupation a person could have.

APRIL 23

Today is Parents Day at Eve's school, so we are getting up early, driving up there, then bringing Eve home for a few days. Unlike seemingly the rest of the world, I'm not a Back to School night, Parent Teacher conferences, Parents Day person.

APRIL 24

I read the newspaper today and thought, This is such a strange time to be alive, the strangest time to be alive in my life.

Henry went to the bat mitzvah of a sixteen-year-old girl, who had, I guess, postponed it for three years because of the pandemic. Eve and I went out late to pick him up. In the car, she brought up the Third Estate, which she is studying in school.

"What's that?" I said, because I have enormous gaps in my knowledge of history. She explained that it was the 98 percent of French people who basically had no rights and no money before the French Revolution.

"People keep having revolutions and nothing changes," she said.

"Yeah," I said.

Revolutions made more sense hundreds of years ago, when there wasn't progress in science and medicine and so many other areas. How are we progressing in those ways and not socially? For me, that is what makes this time the strangest of all.

Oh, and someone stole our trash this week. Yesterday, when I went to put the garbage in our garbage bin outside, I noticed there were no other garbage bags in the bin.

"Someone stole our garbage," I said to Kate as we got in the car to head up to Eve's school.

"What do you mean?" she asked.

"I just put the garbage in the bin and there were no other bags," I said. "Where is our garbage from Tuesday and Wednesday and Thursday?"

"Maybe it's in the wrong bin," she said.

"I don't think so," I said.

Last night, I checked the other bins, and there were no misplaced bags in them, so someone definitely stole our trash. Now we just have to sit here and wait to see what they do with our trash.

Steal our identities? Open up fake credit cards? Or is it possible they were just hungry and hoping for some edible food? I'm not sure what to hope for.

Andrew texted that my cousin Marc says my grandmother's descendants were all from Poland, so now I have all the information on where I'm from. I still don't care.

A few weeks ago, as we were driving to school, Henry asked me, "Do you know what 'Joe Gould's Secret' is?"

"Sure," I said. "It's an essay about a writer named Joe Gould who said he was working on a book for decades and no one knew if the book was real or not."

"Is it good?" he asked.

"I loved it," I said. "It's written by Joseph Mitchell. I read it a million years ago."

"Oh," he said. "I thought it was a just a movie."

"No," I said. "I never saw the movie. I don't think it was good. But the essay was great."

But ever since, I have been wondering if this book is my secret. I mean, I know it exists. But Joe Gould's book could have existed too.

It's just no one saw it. Will anyone see this one or will it be like Joe Gould's? If it is like Joe Gould's, I would like to be able to make my peace with that. It will have one reader, me, but maybe that is okay. Maybe all books have whatever the number of readers it is right for them to have.

APRIL 25

It's 6:00 p.m. I just got off my four o'clock Zoom with Glenn, Max, and Christian. Never in my life have I had a more unpleasant disrespectful meeting. I am literally shaking. I was very kind to all, although occasionally calmly asked Glenn not to use pejorative terms such as "sitcom-y" and "sidekick."

"Claire is a character," I said. "Not a sidekick," referring to Glenn's character's best friend.

At one point, for twenty whole minutes, Glenn pitched out doing an entirely different show that was about her and Pete working together at a Target in Staten Island, then traveling around the middle of the country having "kooky" adventures with people. I think her hope was I would say great and throw out my entire script. Maybe I would be allowed to keep the characters' names.

But nothing else would have anything to do with the scripts I wrote.

At the end, she said, "What do you think?"

"It's a lot to digest," I said. "I'm just going to absorb it."

Then Max swung the conversation back to my script, and for the next hour or so, Glenn and Christian pitched on things that could happen in the show I created.

"What if they have a scene where she shows him her body, just wearing her underwear?" Glenn riffed.

"Maybe," I said, not wanting to point out that as she continued to describe the scene it sounded like a not-as-good version of a scene that my friend Nicole Holofcener wrote for *Lovely & Amazing.*

It was like being in a writers' room on the first day of a season, but sadly, the two people making all the pitches were not writers.

At one point, Glenn pointed out that she knew it was a little odd to be throwing out my entire idea so late in the process.

"But when I heard that new thing in the pitch, that really threw me and I started to rethink everything."

"Glenn," I said. "There was nothing new in the pitch. I did not say one new thing that I hadn't said in a previous meeting."

She looked at me blankly.

"Christian," I said. "Please verify that I said nothing new in the pitch."

He mumbled something to appease Glenn, I can't quite remember what it was because I was upset.

"Christian," I said again. "Please verify that I said nothing new in the pitch."

He again mumbled something meant to appease Glenn.

"Christian," I said for the third time. "Please verify that I said nothing new in the pitch."

"You said nothing new," he mumbled. And we moved on to more ideas from Glenn and Christian.

I kept waiting for the meeting to end, and finally, mercifully, it did. We agreed that we all had had a positive conversation and would now think on all that was said. Christian sent this text after the meeting:

Thanks for spending so much time talking about
the show. This is an awesome show

I wrote back:

Great! I'm excited and energized and hopeful

Which I most certainly was not. Then he wrote back:

Fantastic—I will touch base with Glenn in the
morning. You have Showtime on Wednesday

So I guess this is still happening? I don't know what to think. We literally spent over a half hour justifying to Glenn why this show takes place in the suburbs and not in a city.

There were so many moments like that, where suddenly every aspect of every character was questioned, many of their actions were described by Glenn as "uninteresting" or "not believable."

She would say "That's unbelievable," as if it were a fact.

"That's not a fact, that's an opinion," I said several times. "You may find it unbelievable but another person might not."

"If I don't find it interesting, then I assume everyone will find it uninteresting," she said at one point.

Not necessarily, I thought, but didn't say. I did wonder what the trait of thinking everyone would have the same feeling as you do possibly indicated.

And one more thing—for the entire two hours, Glenn referred to Pete's character as being thirty years younger than her character.

Pete is forty-seven years younger than Glenn, so I think it would be much more accurate to say the character is half a century younger than her once Pete agreed to play him. I am not sure if Glenn literally thinks Pete is thirty years younger than she is, or that she is just not connected to reality.

APRIL 26

Okay, so it is 5:24 p.m. and I have not heard from Christian, Max, Ellyn, Rob, or Laura. So I can safely assume that the Showtime meeting is not happening tomorrow. I am imagining that when Christian checked in with Glenn this morning, she was not excited to move forward with the project, but I have no idea what has actually transpired today.

I can't bring myself to call Ellyn or Rob or Laura. I am assuming they will call me with bad news at 6:15 p.m. like they did a week ago, the night before the HBO Max meeting.

Part of me is strangely relieved, because I now have a very large grudge against Glenn. Or to put it another way, I don't enjoy Glenn. In fact, I think this book should now be named *I Don't Enjoy Glenn Close.*

At one point when she and Christian were pitching ideas yesterday, she said, "Maybe someone cancels Nora for dating Joey."

"That's great," Christian said.

"I hate cancel culture," Glenn said.

"Me too," Christian said. Max and I were silent. Maybe Max likes cancel culture. I know I do. If we didn't have cancel culture, Harvey Weinstein would still be raping people, so just for that, it seems very positive.

6:26 P.M.

Ellyn's assistant just emailed, confirming that the Showtime pitch is happening tomorrow at noon. I am in a state of shock. It feels like there will be another twist in the morning.

APRIL 27

There's a strange bird who has come to live at our house. I hear the noise he or she makes every morning when I wake up around five thirty, and then I hear the noises periodically through the day. No other bird sounds like this bird.

"What's that?" my friend Michelle said when I was in front of the house, talking to her on the phone. "Is that a bird?"

"Yes," I said.

"It sounds so beautiful," she said. The bird has this high-pitched, very short sound it makes over and over again, which sounds like it should be irritating, but there is something almost soothing about it. It's almost as if it comes from such a pure place that it couldn't possibly irritate anyone.

In fact, the bird sounds like a New Zealand bird. Maybe one flew here from New Zealand. I wonder if that is possible.

Henry was coughing before we left for school. He came into the living room and announced that his toothbrush was putting things in his throat.

"It has to be the bristles," I said.

"Yeah," he said. "I think it's the bristles."

"What do you mean, you think?" I asked. "There's nothing else it could be. All a toothbrush could put in your throat are bristles."

"That's why I think it's the bristles," he said.

We went on like that for a while before both of us gave up. I suggested he gargle with hot water.

Kate made the hot water and asked him, "Do you know how to gargle? You gurgle it in your mouth."

I wondered why you don't gargle it in your mouth but chose to be silent. When he gargled, it didn't seem like real gargling, but again, I stayed out of it.

"What's worse?" I asked. "The bristles or brushing with sunscreen?"

"Brushing with sunscreen," he said definitively.

He did his version of gargling a few times but was still coughing, so he took the hot water and got in the car.

He continued to cough as we drove down the hill, so we stopped at the side of the road for him to have some water, then spit it out.

He coughed on and off the whole ride to school, so he occasionally did his version of gargling, which is really just swishing it in his mouth, then spat when we were at stoplights.

Around nine thirty, Christian called to say Pete wasn't able to come to the pitch at noon because he was sick. Pete gets sick a lot, I thought.

Christian had already spoken to Max, and they both thought we should go forward with the pitch. I agreed. It's now 10:33 a.m., and we are still waiting for Glenn to agree to do the pitch without Pete. I say the odds are fifty-fifty on this one.

Also, Christian said he and Glenn had talked a lot about something I said in our Zoom two days ago. Glenn said she wanted to do something subversive, like her Target lady gets a camper idea. I told her that everyone does something subversive for cable/streaming. The real subversive move would be to do something optimistic that gives us hope, because no one ever does that. That really resonated with them, and both are now on board to do my idea, not Glenn's, because of its optimism and hope.

1:25 P.M.

At 11:30 a.m., Glenn texted that she was good to have the meeting without Pete. The meeting went very well.

It began with a short comment by Gary Levine, the person who makes the decision to buy the show and isn't in all meetings.

"We really like this show," he said. "And wanted you to know that."

"Thank you," I said. "And I could sense that, so you didn't need to say anything." Which got a laugh for some reason. I don't even know why I said it.

So I did most of the talking, of course, and I didn't flag any real concerns from the executives.

Amy Israel nodded supportively throughout the meeting, and Gary Levine ended the meeting by thanking all of us for our hard work and said, "I'm excited." I am obviously very surprised, since I was so sure that they would never want it, as it is so unlike their other shows.

Christian and Glenn called after to talk about it. Max was unavailable. Both were very happy with the meeting. I asked what was happening with HBO Max, and Christian said his assistant was currently working on a day and time. But since Glenn has some scheduling issues, I am not sure how realistic it is to think this meeting will happen anytime soon.

Christian reported that Netflix is still very interested and wondering why it is taking so long to find out if they can buy a second script. He said Netflix wants to talk to my lawyer, Dave, who is handling how Sony will be involved.

One more thing—our air-conditioning/heating thing with the panels that need to be taken out is now leaking. So the men who came to our house over and over again a few months ago are now coming back Friday afternoon to see why it is leaking.

Plus, our refrigerator seems to be broken, although it is still working for the moment.

"Let's just burn down the house," I said to Kate, who nodded that yes, that would be for the best.

4:17 P.M.

Haven't heard a word from Showtime. Usually good news comes quicker than this. But there is still hope, just not as much as there was a couple of hours ago.

In the car ride home, Henry said, "There's no way Showtime's buying it."

I explained how well the meeting had gone. "They're not buying it," he said.

Currently, I am nervously baking sugar cookies because I don't know what to do with myself. When the cookies are done, I dip half of each cookie in chocolate and add sprinkles. I started adding these last two steps because I thought it made the cookies exponentially better. Today, I am just grateful for the steps for making the whole process go longer.

APRIL 28

It's 8:45 a.m. Rob, Laura, and Ellyn emailed last night to say they had all contacted Showtime, but no one had heard back.

Hmm.

Also, I got a text from a producer I've worked with in the past named Andrew Singer:

> The Gilligan's Island people called me to say that they think they really blew it by wanting us to audition further for them. They are wondering/ hoping that you're still interested, in which case it's yours/ours. I bet you've moved on creatively and emotionally and I know you also have the Glenn Close/Pete Davidson show . . .

We then texted back and forth and agreed to talk today at two. I had several meetings last year with a large group of descendants of the producer and creator of *Gilligan's Island*. Every time I had a meeting with them, they then said they would all discuss my ideas. Then time would pass and they would ask to have another meeting until finally Andrew decided that it was too challenging a situation to move forward with.

I don't know what I think about revisiting *Gilligan's Island*. I loved the show as a kid but am unclear about how to do it today. On the other hand, maybe Gilligan can save me from Glenn.

7:32 P.M.

I spent all day wandering around, waiting to hear from Showtime. At two, I spoke with Andrew about *Gilligan's Island*. We talked about it for about twenty minutes, then agreed we should go forward with trying to sell it to Peacock, who he has already spoken to about the project. We decided he should have one more phone call with the agent representing the families who have the rights, to make sure they are okay to not be involved with the show creatively and to just let us do what we want.

Andrew is producing the other Pete Davidson show. He told me that Netflix and Amazon both offered a one-season commitment after reading the script and hearing a pitch, but they went with Peacock, which offered a two-season commitment.

That's a lot more than Netflix offered us, I thought.

Andrew described the opening sequence of their show in which the audiences sees Pete masturbating. Then his mother walks in on him just as he is about to ejaculate and he ejaculates on her.

"Dinner's ready," she says.

Oh boy, I thought, I should just retire.

Later, I picked up Henry, and he asked about Showtime. "I haven't heard anything," I said.

"That's great," he said.

"Why?" I said.

"I would have thought they would have said no by now. This means they're actually considering it."

Then, minutes later, I looked at my phone at a stoplight. There was a text from Laura at CAA. The light turned green and I asked Henry to read me the text. He said that Showtime loved the pitch and were giving the script to two higher-up executives because they knew they would need to come through with a bigger commitment given the talent involved.

Maybe it will end up at Showtime after all. I would definitely prefer that to Netflix. I'm still waiting to hear when we go to HBO Max. I am sure there is a story as to why this meeting hasn't been set yet. Supposedly, people are being fired at HBO Max, so maybe that has something to do with it.

APRIL 29

I was bringing the recycling out as the van from the heating/air-conditioning place pulled up. Two men got out, one of whom looked like he might have been here before.

"Hi," I said to him, unsure if it was him because when he was here a few months ago, he was mostly wearing a mask. "Have you been here before?"

"Yes, I have," he said. "Three or four times."

We laughed and went inside, and I explained the problem. I left him and went to the laundry room.

"Shoot," I heard him say.

It's not the kind of situation where you want to hear someone say "Shoot." I came back into the hall.

He gestured toward the removable panel. "I forgot I needed the tool for these."

I then searched through the very few tools we have while he went back to the van to look for it there. Neither of us had the tool.

"I'm going to have to come back," he said.

"Yes," I said, and smiled. "You always do,"

He smiled back at me, then said the office would call me to reschedule another visit. Then he left.

So we are back in it again.

APRIL 30

We went to our friends Joe and Mary's for drinks last night. They asked about the Glenn project, and I brought them up-to-date. They looked horrified by my story. I told them about the opening scene of the other Pete project.

"We should all just quit the business," Joe said.

"I could make anyone quit the business," I said. They all agreed that after talking for five minutes to me, anyone would quit the business.

Mary had a story about one of the higher-up Showtime executives that doesn't bode well for me. She was pitching a show to him and he kept asking who one character was fucking. She would then pivot to other people the other characters were having sex with, but he kept asking about the first character, "But who's she fucking?"

Mary then told another story about someone who pitched a documentary about Putin to this executive.

At the end of the pitch, he said, "You know what interests me? Who's Putin fucking?"

As my project is a romantic *Moonstruck* kind of piece, I'm not sure he's the ideal person to be deciding its fate at Showtime this weekend.

MAY 1

I just laid down on the ground for a half hour. It's supposed to help with anxiety, inflammation, your heart, and a million other things.

I don't know if it did do those things, but it was pleasant, mostly because I was very conscious of the smell of grass.

It's a smell I associate with mowing the lawn when I was a kid. We had a nonelectric lawn mower, like most people I knew. When you had a nonelectric lawn mower, you really went to battle with the lawn, and I definitely remember there were times when the lawn won.

I wish I could go to a museum show of the artifacts of my childhood. I would love to wander around looking at things like a hand eggbeater. I used our hand eggbeater religiously, as if eggs could never be beaten without one or whatever you were making would not taste good at all. Now I see no real use for an eggbeater whatsoever. I wonder who still uses them.

I don't eat hard-boiled eggs ever, and rarely did in childhood, but I remember we had a hard-boiled egg slicer, something I have never seen since then.

When we sold my father's house, mostly everything went into dumpsters. Instead, I should have gone around collecting items for the artifacts of my childhood museum show.

MAY 2

It's a Silent Monday. It's almost 1:00 p.m. and I haven't heard anything about Showtime.

Kate heard Henry coughing after he brushed his teeth this morning.

"Are you still swallowing bristles?" she asked.

"Yes," he said.

"But we got you a new toothbrush," she said.

"I know," he said. It was determined one of us would watch him brush his teeth to figure out why this might be happening.

On the way to school, Henry wanted to listen to the score of *Company*. We watched the documentary about the making of the original cast album a while back, and it really had an impact on him. The other day, he said that is what made him want to be a playwright. Ironically, George Furth, who wrote the book of *Company*, is on-screen for maybe five seconds and barely speaks. But as Henry explained it, his wanting to be a playwright had nothing to do with George Furth and everything to do with Stephen Sondheim.

Watching Sondheim create something theatrically made him interested in the theater in a way that he isn't in films or television. I am not sure why, exactly. It just seems to have inspired him in a way that he couldn't quite put into words or that I couldn't quite understand.

As we listened to the songs today, I was jealous of all the people who got to work on the original production of *Company*. A half hour later, I was at the gym and passed by a television, which had on the *Today* show. Glenn was a guest, publicizing the Apple TV show she did last year. When I looked at her face, I felt sick to my stomach, which may sound strong but is exactly how I felt.

After our conversation a week ago where she was extremely demeaning, I just don't look forward to working with her. To be honest, it is not just not a feeling of not looking forward to working with her. I saw something that scared me.

I wish I was working with the actors who were in the original production of *Company*, I thought as I watched Glenn beaming a wide smile at some *Today* host.

After the gym, I didn't know what to do with myself, so I had another UCLA botanical garden/sculpture garden morning.

An old college friend called me while I was walking on the campus, and I told him everything that had happened since we last spoke over a week ago.

"I really hate her," he said about Glenn. Then he said everything would be fine if this does keep moving forward, which who knows if it will.

After I left UCLA, I went to buy more Ping-Pong balls, then went to Diesel Bookstore and didn't find anything to buy. I used to read constantly and now I barely read. Mostly I read old books, but now that I think about it, I did read about a new book I wanted to buy, but now have no idea what it was. I don't know why I went to Diesel, since clearly there is no way I would be able to commit to a book on a waiting-to-hear-from-Showtime day.

Now I am home and am going to bounce on the mini-trampoline for twenty minutes, then lie on the ground for a half hour. I'm actually enjoying today in a way I often don't on Silent Mondays.

MAY 3

I am in the middle of doing laundry. A few minutes ago, when I went to the area in the back of the house where the washer and dryer are, I heard a bad noise coming from the washing machine.

Shit, I thought. Then I saw an enormous pool of water in the hall. I turned the corner, and water was pouring out of the washing machine. I stopped it and opened it to find some piece of clothing had attacked the rubbery circle thing that keeps water in. Or at least I think that is what its function is. I guess its function is obvious to most people, but of course not at all obvious to me.

While I was doing battle with the clothing and the rubbery thing, I screamed loudly at the top of my lungs. In fact, it wasn't just one scream. It went on for some time.

I put the rubbery thing back where it is supposed to be, but there seems to be a big wire thing that got dislodged. So now I am doing another quick cycle to get all the sopping wet clothing a little less sopping wet. It is all very tenuous, but it seems to be working for the moment.

So now we have to get the washing machine fixed. The roofer is coming tomorrow to look at the leaks. I have to call a heater-repair place because no one has called me to reschedule about the air-conditioning/heater leak. Plus, there is the refrigerator, specifically it's the refrigerator door, which has a a bad gasket. In fact, now that I think about it, this washing machine broken piece would seem to be another bad gasket.

On the bright side, the laundry area floor is now really clean where the pool of water formerly was. There is always an upside to something breaking—you clean someplace in a way you never would normally.

Earlier today, I finally heard from Laura about Showtime:

> Jessie said Showtime is still working on what the offer is going to look like, but they love it and think it could be a perfect fit. They are meeting to discuss further on Thursday. Well done!!

My friend Rachel reminded me of something that I knew already but had clearly forgotten—this situation with Glenn is an opportunity for me to grow. We talked about how hate isn't making my life any easier. In fact, my life would be a lot easier if I weren't filled with hate.

Rachel pointed out that I should just focus on getting what I want from the situation. So that is what I will do. Or try to do, more realistically.

MAY 4

The roofer is here now, walking around on the roof, as I type this. He is a large man, and I am a little concerned that he is too large for the roof, as everything in the house seems overly delicate currently.

"Do you think he is too large for the roof?" I just whispered to Kate.

"Obviously, I wondered," she said, then added, "I think this happened last time too."

He is stomping around very confidently, so hopefully as a roofer he has enough knowledge of roofs to know that he is not too large to be stomping around up there.

I got an email from Ellyn's assistant at the end of the day yesterday:

Hi Bruce,

Would 5/9 at 4pm PT work for you for the pitch with HBO Max?
Thanks

I was surprised. I had started to assume that there would be no HBO Max meeting, since no one had mentioned it for days and days. Usually, canceled meetings get rescheduled within a day or two after they are canceled.

Also, I got this text from Kate Berlant at the end of the day:

BRUCE. john is now getting surgery on the 10th, thank God. We hand in our special the 13th. I'm on a movie every week day of may. Realistically, we are looking at june to buckle down, but I will have downtime on set and we would love to at least get on the phone in may after we are done with the special. We miss you!!!

I texted back:

Great

Miss you too!

At this point I assume that the Kate-and-John project is never actually happening, as we have been in conversation for months upon months and have not moved forward in any way. But who knows? I didn't think Showtime would ever be the right place for the Glenn-and-Pete project.

I have been thinking a lot about what Rachel said about hate and the effect it has on me as I go through the day. I notice it each time it comes up and try not to succumb to it.

There was traffic on the way to school today, and I had hate for the driver of a car up ahead of me that I felt should have been moving forward and wasn't. I honked maniacally.

"What does that do?" Henry said.

"I'm expressing my emotional truth," I said.

"Hmm," he barely uttered, seemingly unconvinced.

Anyhow, this was a case of succumbing, as I am well aware. But later at the gym, I was on a stationary bicycle and noticed that the man in front of me was watching Fox News on his stationary bicycle.

I instinctively was filled with hate for him. Then decided instead to see him as a scared child. And actually, it wasn't just seeing. I truly experienced him as a scared child. I noticed how much better my body felt when I experienced him this way. And I managed to continue to experience him that way whenever I would see him for the rest of my time at the gym.

5:13 P.M.

A man came to fix the washer this afternoon. He wasn't successful and is going to come back. After he left, I didn't know what to do with myself, so I laid on the ground for a half hour, then I made the tomato and fennel soup.

As I was preparing the fennel and tomatoes and onions and garlic to be roasted, the pan fell on the ground, and as everything was covered in olive oil, it was a mess. I washed everything off and reapplied the olive oil, but I am hoping no one gets sick from everything falling on the floor. Since everything was so oily, I then had to mop the floor. I guess I am cracking up a little bit under the strain of this Glenn-and-Pete project. Now that it is getting closer to actually happening, I am starting to get more unhinged. It is somewhat similar to the feeling of having to urinate while you are driving home and then, when you get a couple of blocks from home, you suddenly feel like you can't hold it in anymore.

I can't hold in my Glenn-and-Pete project stress anymore. It is just too unbearable.

MAY 5

It's Thursday, the day Showtime is supposedly meeting to decide what the offer is. I am having a hard time concentrating, so I am looking up black bean and kale recipes, none of which look that good, but maybe it is my mood.

I just texted Andrew Singer to see if he talked to the UTA agent about *Gilligan's Island*. He texted that they keep missing each other, but will try him again today.

I then texted:

Was it pushy to ask?

He didn't respond, so maybe it was. I'm just sitting here, waiting for the heater-repair people. I am not confident that this will be their last trip to fix this leak.

Ten minutes after my text, Andrew wrote back:

Not at all

And then ten minutes later, he wrote:

On with him now. He says he will protect you from
having any notes from them. He asked that we do
one "reconnect" zoom with just Ross Schwartz, Tracy
(his wife's aunt), and himself . . . they will be the
emissarys who will then tell the rest of the family's
they are going with you/us and have given us their
blessing. If you're open to that, I'll set it up.

I wrote back:

Ok

Then realized that might be confusing so added:

I mean I'm very open!

4:25 P.M.

Still haven't heard anything, and the heater-repair people never showed up. I just called them and they said I wasn't on the schedule. I feel like I will never be on any schedule. After we talked for a while, the heater-repair lady did see I was on the schedule, but for some reason the technicians never showed up. She says they will come tomorrow at three.

I've cleaned everywhere, washed both of our cars, done laundry, and soon will start making a southwestern black bean kale sweet potato skillet.

Henry and I have been listening to *A Chorus Line* on the way to and from school. My friend Gary wrote about it in a chapter of his new book, and he talked about it at a book event the other night. Henry already knew it was Kate's and my favorite musical, but he was especially curious to listen to it after Gary talked about it.

The pain of the characters in *A Chorus Line* is so profound and almost too much to bear. I can't believe how lucky we were to be kids and have *A Chorus Line* to see and listen to over and over again.

Once, shortly after I moved to Los Angeles, I found myself at a Hamilton High School production of *A Chorus Line*. Hamilton High is like the school in *Fame*, which I also feel lucky to have had come out when I was a kid, although in no way, shape, or form am I putting it in the same category as *A Chorus Line*. I loved *Fame* as a kid but knew it wasn't as layered, complex, and soulful as *A Chorus Line.*

Anyway, because these kids really did want to become performers professionally and were probably scared that they would not make it, their performances were so real, almost too real. That night in that high school theater was one of the best nights I have had in any theater. I'll never forget what those kids did that night onstage. It was the most palpably painful and exquisite production of *A Chorus Line* that you could ever see.

No one should ever see the movie version of *A Chorus Line.* I saw it in the theater in New York City when I was in college I think, or right after. The woman who played Cassie was so, so awful that when she climbed to the top of a ladder during some bad number, someone in the audience yelled out, "Jump!" I've always loved whoever that person in the audience was, and to me, that person was a real true New Yorker.

MAY 6

So . . . there is not going to be an offer from Showtime this week. A little after ten this morning, I got a text from Ellyn on the chain with Laura and Rob:

> Bruce, it's not official but . . . Amy Israel told
> Lauren Fox that Showtime is making a pilot
> production commitment.

> Meanwhile, Dave Ryan has been in it with Netflix
> BA, connecting them to Sony BA.

Things are moving!

Laura wrote:

Yes! Super exciting. More clarity next week.

Rob wrote:

Here we goooo

I wrote:

Ok

A few hours later, I got an email from Andrew Singer's assistant, whose name is Austin Matloff, which I think is a great name.

Austin offered me some times next week to meet with Andrew and the *Gilligan's Island* people. I took the first available time and day, Wednesday at 11:00 a.m.

It is now 2:09 p.m. and the heater-repair people are here working on the air conditioner leak. Let's see how they do.

And I just got an email about the Monday HBO Max pitch from Christian's assistant:

Hi Bruce,

We still haven't heard from Pete's team, but Christian said to go ahead and set it without him and hopefully he'll be able to make it. Below are the meeting details for 5/9 @ 4p PT!

2:34 P.M.

Because the workers left the front door open to come in and out of the house, a bee was in the living room. Henry has severe bee allergies, so

I couldn't have any peace of mind while the bee was in the house. I opened the sliding back door and hoped the bee would leave through either of the open doors. When he didn't, I needed a weapon to kill him. We don't have any newspapers or magazines, so I went out to our recycling bin to get a catalog, rolled it up, and came back in. We were in a battle for about ten minutes or so, but in the end, I killed him with the rolled-up catalog. It was the highlight of my day.

Now that I think about it, a rolled-up magazine is one of the simplest and most elegant and effective weapons in the world. When I saw that bee, I instinctively knew what was needed. I was lucky we had catalogs to use in lieu of a magazine or newspaper, which we used to have tons of but now have none of.

When the catalogs stop coming, which I assume they will eventually, I won't be able to re-create my elegant weapon.

Henry and Eve probably have no idea that this weapon even exists. Maybe it won't by the time they are adults.

Kate buys fly swatters, which I find odd. A fly swatter is a worse version of a rolled-up catalog.

3:26 P.M.

The heater-repair men just left, saying that it is all fixed. "What was the problem?" I asked.

One mumbled something about how the previous men hadn't put a good enough drain in.

"Now it works," he said very loudly and confidently.

I wonder. Whatever they did, it sounded like it involved a ton of masking tape. I kept hearing the masking tape sound for at least fifteen minutes.

I wish I had more faith in everything. In a way, it is easier for me to have faith in a macro sense, rather than a micro. It seems like nothing works out in the micro, but everything works out in the macro.

I'm making vegan Caesar dressing because Eve is coming home

tonight and she usually wants it. The mustard was almost gone and there was no backup mustard like there usually is. I scraped and scraped the jar until I finally got almost a tablespoon, which is what I needed. I did one last scrape and the tablespoon slipped out of my hand and landed on the floor, spilling all the mustard out of it. I'd already gone to Vicente Foods once today, so you know what that means.

MAY 7

This email came in from Rob at CAA at the end of the day yesterday:

> Hey Bruce—I've been talking to the producers of *Life & Beth* about writers for season 2 and they have asked to meet with you. They're thinking about a 7/25 start. The three of us spoke and think you should 100% take this meeting. Not sure if you've watched it but both Laura and I love it and it has had a great critical reception. This a great show and think it would be a real value add, if it worked out.
>
> Of course even with a production order for the Glenn project, we obviously don't know how things are going to shake out with the timing given Glenn/Pete/Max's schedules, so I would suggest you take it as we see how everything with the Glenn project plays out. We can always carve it out if we need too!

I took a screenshot of his email and texted it to my friends Sarah and Max. Sarah wrote:

> It's very threatening

I wrote back:

Yes it is

When I didn't want to meet on *Reboot*, Ellyn said it was okay. But in an ominous tone of voice, she'd added that it did mean that it would be harder to not meet on the next staffing job. So here we are.

We all watched the first two episodes of the first season of *Life & Beth* last night. Henry left the room in disgust.

"Amy Schumer's not funny," he said on his way out. Eve did homework. Kate and I were mildly engaged.

At least it's sort of intelligent, I thought. It's not embarrassing. So far, that is my official position on *Life & Beth*—it's not embarrassing.

MAY 8

It's Sunday night. It was nice having Eve home and I was very sad to drop her off back at school.

There was a lot of traffic on the way back to Carpinteria, but I didn't mind. The beach looked so beautiful and the classical music we were listening to was also so beautiful and I was just grateful to have had my weekend and not to be living in Ukraine or a small MAGA town somewhere.

If the kids get into Fieldston, we will live full-time with Eve again, which is one of the main reasons I would like them to get in. I wonder if we will hear something from Fieldston this week. I know both Henry and Eve are thinking about it a lot and will be extremely disappointed if they don't get in.

We watched another *Life & Beth* last night. I want to take a break from watching tonight, but then I am just going to have to go back to it, so maybe I have to watch at least one tonight. I don't know how I am going to slog through the rest of the episodes. I'm praying there are only eight of them. If there are ten, I will kill myself.

I just checked. There are ten episodes.

MAY 9

We didn't watch *Life & Beth* last night. Instead we finished an old Ida Lupino film noir I had never seen called *Woman in Hiding*. It was strange, but the three of us all loved it.

Kate is going out tonight. On the way to school, Henry asked me, "What are we going to watch tonight?"

"I don't know," I said.

"But not *Life & Beth*?" he said, clearly worried that could be a possibility.

"No," I said. I am probably just going to have to watch some episodes during the day tomorrow.

Today, I am preparing for my pitch with HBO Max at four. I hate late-afternoon pitches, as that means I am just filled with dread all day long.

Christian called this morning to say he isn't able to be in the pitch because of a doctor's appointment for a hernia problem. He doesn't want to postpone the pitch because Pete has tentatively said he would be able to make it. Let's see if he does.

4:00 P.M.

I got a call from Ellyn's office that HBO Max wants to know if we can do it at 4:30. I said I was fine with that.

Ten minutes before that, Ellyn and Laura called to say that Pete wasn't going to be able to make the meeting, which I was also fine with.

7:21 P.M.

The meeting ended at 5:08, which is a little short.

Suzanna, the executive in charge, interrupted me midway as I pitched the season out and asked what the last episode was. I am choosing to think it is not because she was bored and wanted the pitch to end, but because she needed to go to whatever her next meeting was, which obviously also had been pushed.

In any case, I would say the meeting went well, as there were only positive things said by the executives. Suzanna ended the meeting by saying she wanted to read the pilot again because so much time has passed since she read it the first time, and then I guess they will decide whether or not to make an offer. But I haven't heard anything back from the agents or from Christian, so I don't really know how the meeting went. Great meetings can always end up being terrible meetings.

At the end of the day, there were a lot of texts from Rob, Laura, and Ellyn about *Life & Beth*.

Rob wrote:

Open to a meeting?

I wrote back:

I'm 3 in. I'd like to keep watching.

Rob wrote back:

Because you love it so much???

I wrote back:

No

Then there was a flurry of texts from all about how good the credit would be and how much I needed to take this meeting. I will spare you those. They definitely wouldn't be fun for me to type out.

MAY 10

It's a little after three and I haven't heard anything from anyone about how the HBO Max meeting went, and, of course, still haven't heard what Showtime's offer is. It's a waiting day.

Saturday is my friend Sarah's wedding, where I am going to read something during the ceremony. The first thing that occurred to me to read was to find something that had the sentence "This is the perfect day" in it and see if the rest of whatever I found was also appropriate. But when I googled that, all I could find was an Avril Lavigne song that had that sentence in it. I thought about reading the lyrics out loud at the wedding, but that seemed like a bad idea.

So I gave up on that phrase and started to think about who were my favorite writers. Then I thought, I'm one of my favorite writers, so I decided to write something. I didn't know what I was going to write until I found myself saying something about Eve's volleyball team to Sarah on the phone and knew that was the perfect thing to write, and here it is:

> My name is Bruce and I am a girls volleyball club parent. A month or two ago I was talking to Sarah and telling her something I noticed at one of my daughter Eve's tournaments.
>
> I should tell you first that Eve's club is very highly ranked and they win a lot of games. And there are some extremely good athletes on her team.

But during this tournament, they were playing another team and I noticed something striking. Eve's team plays like individuals, and sometimes that doesn't get in their way. But a lot of times it does. They go for a ball when they should be letting someone closer go for it. Or they all gravitate toward one area, leaving another area unprotected. The team they were playing against played like they were a perfect unit. They never all went for a ball or left any open areas.

Every move they made was designed to work in tandem with each other. And that is what made them win the tournament. They clearly knew how to work together so they can go all the way.

After I told Sarah, she said "You should write that as a movie. That could be your sports movie." As it happens, I hate sports so I am not going to write it as a sports movie. Although anyone listening now can option it. See me after the ceremony.

But I did write it as something to read at this wedding. Because a few weeks ago, I was visiting Sarah and Aaron, and as I observed them, I got the same feeling I got from the other team. Sarah and Aaron are a perfect unit. And just like the other team, it is a joy to behold. [Editor's note: Kate made me add a sentence here after she read it that I think is a network note but I still put it in: And maybe that's what ideally a marriage should be—a perfect unit.] So in my opinion Sarah and Aaron could win any girls volleyball tournament in Southern California. Or do anything else they want to do. They clearly know how to go all the way.

So that is what I am going to read on Saturday. I hope they like it.

MAY 11

Oh boy. It's another no news from anyone/watching *Life & Beth* day. I am on episode seven. If I have to have another no news from anyone/watching *Life & Beth* day tomorrow, I will kill myself.

The washer repairman who was here last week just came back, and now we have a new washing machine gasket.

5:46 P.M.
Henry and Eve got into Fieldston. They are excited beyond belief, and Kate and I are freaking out—we are moving to New York. It's very overwhelming.

I decided to power through and am now on the tenth and last episode of *Life & Beth*. There are some good scenes in the last few episodes, but it still feels so derivative, and what's the point? But I am not sure what I am going to say to Laura, Rob, and Ellyn.

6:11 P.M.
Only eleven minutes left of the last *Life & Beth*. Henry just walked into the room and I told him I was almost done watching all ten episodes.

"It's like I've climbed Mount Everest," I said.

"Yes," he said.

"In fact, it's like I've climbed two Mount Everests," I said.

"With none of the reward," Henry said.

"None at all," I said. "It's just made me question how I could have wasted so much precious time."

"I understand," he said.

MAY 12

I wrote to Henry's and Eve's schools to say that they would not be coming back in the fall. When Henry's school responded, I some-how felt a huge wave of relief, and since then, I have been giddy with excitement. I actually feel ten years younger, excited for what the future will bring. It's quite a surprising reaction.

I texted Rob, Laura, and Ellyn that I would meet on *Life & Beth*. I am not sure I want to do it for a variety of reasons, but they want me to take the meeting, so I will at least do that.

I then asked if we had heard any news from Showtime or HBO Max. Laura responded:

Showtime is making an offer today or tomorrow.
And we just spoke w Suzanna Makkos who is
unfortunately passing. She made it clear
she is not buying much right now in the
merger.

I wrote back:

Ok thanks

It was slightly disappointing, and yet . . . it was sort of a relief. A lot of Suzanna's questions and thoughts were sort of perplexing, and I was nervous about that. Although in theory I did prefer to be at HBO Max, her questions didn't bode well for the future cre-atively for the show, and gave me a queasy feeling.

Rob then texted that the Showtime higher-up who wants to know who Putin's fucking is a big supporter of the project. He also wrote:

There is a lot of love for it at Showtime!

And I think honestly for the best at Max . . . it's going to be a tough place to get anything made (especially anything that isn't dirt cheap) for the immediate time being

So that is that. Looks like it will be going to Showtime, although there has still been no offer.

MAY 13

Still no offer from Showtime. I have been running around, getting things done today, and am now packing frantically before we go to pick Henry up at school and then go to Ojai for Sarah and Aaron's wedding.

I turned on the air conditioner, which I haven't used since before heater-repair people came. It's not leaking, but it is making a very unusual and slightly alarming sound.

I talked to my friend Jen earlier today. We were catching up on various things.

"I can't stop reading about Ukraine," she said. "Especially the Ukrainians."

"I'm sure," I said. "It's because they're so inspiring."

"Yes," she said, then added a little more quietly, "I hadn't put it into words."

"They show that there is still good in the world. And that good can still fight back. The Ukrainians mean we can still hope."

"Yes," she said again.

MAY 14

The offer from Showtime was forwarded to me last night while we were at the night-before-the-wedding dinner in Ojai.

The gist seems to be that the offer is to shoot a pilot, but before they pull the trigger on that, I need to rewrite the first episode and give them a second episode. So that is a little disappointing, in that it seems conditional, as opposed to just committing to shoot the pilot. But maybe I am not understanding it in some way.

MAY 15

We got home from Sarah's wedding about an hour ago. I am now doing laundry. Last night, I was in an otherworldly place in Ojai, eating and drinking at a long table artfully decorated with crystals and scented candles and dried flowers. And now I am on the floor sorting the lights from the darks. I often feel like Cinderella. It really is the most relatable of the fairy tales, I think. Haven't we all had magical evenings then mere hours later are dealing with the drudgery of life?

Although in truth, my household chores don't feel much like drudgery, more like things that ground me.

Only moments after we arrived home, I took out the garbage. When I opened up the black bin outside, it was empty. There should have been at least four garbage bags in there. So someone has stolen our garbage for the second time. Who wants our garbage?

I was very nervous before my reading at the wedding, but Sarah seemed happy with it, and after the ceremony, a lot of people said nice things to me about it. I am so glad it is over now and it seems like it will be an eternity before I am ever asked to speak again at a wedding.

There was a lot of traffic on the way up Friday. Because the ride was so long, we stopped at a car dealership for Kate and Henry to go to the bathroom. I called my friend Max, who was already in Ojai.

"It's so hot," I said.

"It's boiling here," he said. I couldn't imagine that it could be hotter than at the dealership, but when I got there, it was. Max was dead right. I felt like I was being boiled.

The sun was setting by the time we got to the night-before-the-wedding dinner for all the guests.

The next day, we all got in a shuttle to go to the wedding, which was to take place at three o'clock.

On the shuttle, my friend Natalie and her husband, Zach, were sitting in front of us.

I told Natalie an offer from Showtime had come in last night.

"Let me see the offer," she said. I handed her my phone and she looked it over. She is a television executive at Imagine.

She asked a few questions about it, and Zach, a talent agent at CAA, said, "Let me see it."

She handed the phone to Zach, and he studied the deal.

"It's pay or play," he said, and then there was some talk of what pay or play actually meant. He kept saying it meant that money was taken out of Showtime and put in a separate account, and I kept saying, "Doesn't it just mean that they will pay me, Glenn, Max, and Pete whether they make the pilot or not?"

Both things seemed to be true, but his final words were, "It seems as if they are going to be out a lot of money if they pay everyone without making it, so I think they're going to make it."

That was reassuring. Then my friend Jenni, who was sitting behind me on the shuttle, leaned forward.

"Good luck finding shade at this," she said, because she knows how much I hate the sun.

"I'm sure there will be some shade," I said.

The shuttle struggled a bit to get to our destination, but a short time later we were dropped off at what seemed to be a tiny farm outside Ojai. It was a million degrees.

"There's some shade," I said. But there really wasn't much. And a couple of hours later, we all were summoned to the area where long tables were set for us to sit down and have dinner.

There was no shade at the tables. So it was boiling hot and there was no shade and it was still the best wedding ever. In fact, the boiling heat made the experience even better.

It reminded me of my college graduation. It was many, many years ago and I don't remember much about it, but it was so hot that the memory of that day is permanently etched in my body. I think back about my high school graduation and I can access it a little bit, but I think back to my college graduation and it is as if I am actually there.

I think it will be the same way with this wedding. Decades from now, if I am alive decades from now, I will think back to Sarah's wedding, and it will be as if I am there again, on that wonderful day, in the boiling heat.

And while we are on the subject of weddings, I want to say one more thing. There is a scene I love in *Giant*, a movie that I don't really love. Elizabeth Taylor and Rock Hudson are I believe having some kind of rough moment in their marriage and are very alienated from each other. They arrive at a wedding and while they are watching the ceremony, they reconnect to who they were on their wedding day, and whatever alienation with each other they are feeling disappears.

Ever since I married Kate, every single time we have gone to a wedding, there is always one moment during the ceremony, usually during the vows, when I look at her and think, oh, it's you, the only person I would ever want to be married to and the only person I would ever want to spend my life with.

I actually remember waking up on the morning of our wedding day and thinking marrying Kate is the most right decision I have ever made and it was. Nothing, but nothing, has ever felt more right. It's a good feeling.

MAY 16

It's five thirty. It's been a very Silent Monday. And a very unusual day.

Before I left the house to take Henry to school, a caption for a cartoon popped into my head. I haven't drawn a cartoon in over two years. I stopped a few weeks before the pandemic came to the United States in March 2020. Even before that, when I was drawing cartoons, captions rarely popped into my head.

Usually I sat down at my desk and I would start drawing, and then captions would come. Or if I was on a set or on a plane or had a few minutes to spare out in the world, I would write ideas down in a notebook, and captions would come out of those.

I dropped Henry off at school and went to the gym. When I was on the stationary bicycle, I thought, maybe I should just do cartoons today, and soon, ideas started coming to me and I typed them into in my phone.

Then I went home and told Kate that I was going to draw cartoons. She smiled widely.

"Things are really shifting," she said.

I sat down at my desk and started drawing. My hand was a little unsteady at first and I felt a little unsteady in my head. But within moments, I got lost in the cartoons.

A couple of hours later, I went into the living room and showed some cartoons to Kate, and she was very positive.

Then I texted Max and Sarah:

I did cartoons for the first time in over 2 years today

Can I run them by the Buchmans

That is the name of our text chain. Sarah replied:

Yes

So I sent them. Then waited for them to respond. Neither responded for almost a half hour and I was nervous they were awful and they didn't know what to say. Finally, Max wrote:

I'm thrilled you're back at it
Love all of them especially Toni Collette and Covid

Sarah quickly responded:

Me too

Same favorites

And then I sent them to the *New Yorker* for this week's art meeting. It has been so long. I wonder what they will say.

I am not sure what happened to make me do this. Over the years, various people have registered sadness that I stopped drawing the cartoons, as if some piece of me had died. And maybe they were right. But before this morning, I had absolutely no desire to draw one again. I assumed I never would.

So what exactly did shift? I am not sure, but I wonder if it is connected to a conversation I had on Saturday.

About ten minutes after the wedding ceremony, I noticed Sarah's mother talking to one of her grandchildren. I went over to them, and we talked about Sarah and Aaron and the ceremony. Her grandchild wandered off and now we were alone.

"How has today been for you?" I found myself asking her.

"Hard," she said. "And thank you for asking." We discussed why it was hard for her, and I said, "Look, everyone has certain things that are hard for them. This is yours."

"Yes," she said, looking relieved. Then she said, "I love your drawings."

She told me about how Sarah had saved the birthday card I drew for her daughter, Juniper.

"It was just a little drawing," I said.

"There's just something special about how you draw," she said. It was just the smallest of exchanges, but it seems to have unlocked something.

But as I said, I have had this kind of exchange fairly often with people over the last two years, so maybe it was the accumulation of them that unlocked something.

Or maybe things get mysteriously unlocked, and we don't know why they do and can't ever know why.

MAY 17

A few days ago, I was on the stationary bike at the gym of the hotel we were staying at for the weekend in Ojai. I looked over at a woman with a crazed smile who was on another stationary bike. It was Maria Shriver.

I then left the gym, got a cup of coffee, then went back to the gym and got back on the same bike.

My friend Deb saw me through the window and came in, excitedly.

"We just did yoga with Maria Shriver," she said. It is the kind of thing that makes Deb happy and it makes anyone who knows Deb happy that this is the kind of thing that makes her happy.

Jenni then came in and looked at me. "You're still on the bike?" she said. She knows I have a tendency to overexercise.

"I went and did other things, then came back," I said.

I have for a long time had a big grudge against Maria Shriver. So I then told Jenni and Deb about the grudge.

I never had any feelings about her until her husband, Arnold Schwarzenegger, was running for governor of California. Maria was friends with Oprah, and in the final months of his campaign, Maria got her and Arnold an hour with Oprah on her TV show. This hour of television really humanized him and I feel helped this person get elected. Whenever I would see Maria's face on television, I would be sickened.

Years passed. When Irving Lazar died, he had a big funeral with many famous people. There was a list of who was invited to the funeral. Because I had worked for Irving and his wife, Mary, I was considered sort of part family/part former worker, so I was asked to be the person at the entrance with the guest list to make sure people who drove in were on it.

Only one person tried to get in who wasn't on the list. It was Maria Shriver. When she drove up, I looked for her name.

"I'm sorry," I said. "You're not on the list."

Finally, I had my payback. It only lasted five minutes. Somehow she got someone else to let her drive in. But still. I did get the five minutes, and that was something.

Ellyn, Rob, Laura, and I had a conference call with my lawyers, Patti and Dave, to talk about the two offers from Showtime and Netflix. Everyone acknowledges it seems like this show will go to Showtime in the end, but they want to negotiate with both to see how that will impact the other.

"Is there any way Netflix will want to match what Showtime is offering?" I asked.

There was a silence. Then someone, I think it was Laura, said, "Netflix laid off a hundred and fifty people today. I don't think they are going to match Showtime's offer."

At the end of the call, I asked everyone if it was still possible to shoot this pilot in September when Pete becomes available and before Max Barbakow becomes unavailable in November. No one would give me any real answer, so it is looking like that answer might be no.

MAY 18

I woke up this morning, sick to my stomach about moving to New York in six weeks or so. This may be the craziest move I have ever made.

Last night was a primary night, so I have a bad feeling about that too. So many election deniers won their primaries. What is going to happen when these insane people are elected, as many of them seemingly will be?

I drew cartoons early this morning, before anyone else in the house woke up. It made me think of Liana, who I have been putting off calling. I was hoping she would text me that her agent read and loved her pilot, but she never did.

A few weeks ago, Laura from CAA told me that she had read Liana's pilot and loved it but didn't think there was a buyer for it out there in the marketplace.

"They all want Seth MacFarlane–type shows," she said, which this most definitely is not.

I relayed that information to Liana this morning. "Should I make it more like *Family Guy*?" she said.

"No," I said. "What you wrote is wonderful and there is no way to make it more like *Family Guy*."

I told her I had started drawing cartoons again.

"I'm so glad," she said. "Is it fun to do after being away? That's how it is for me."

"Uh," I said, thinking about whether it was fun or not. When you have to think about it, I guess the answer is not really. But I said, "It's everything, I think. Fun and not fun."

"Oh," she said, seemingly not able to have an answer to that.

I'm having an anxious making-lots-of-things-in-the-kitchen day. I am about to make avocado hummus for the first time. I just realized I have my *Gilligan's Island* meeting in two days and have nothing new to say about it. I just texted Andrew Singer:

> Do I have to say anything new at this meeting on
> Friday?

A short while later, Andrew wrote back:

> Nah

So I guess I won't try to think of anything new to say. Not having to say anything new is the best possible feeling.

MAY 19

I mostly worked on cartoons for next week's meeting today. It's strange how I've just fallen back into it, after not doing it for so long. When I submitted the cartoons on Monday, I wrote:

> I know, I know
> It's been a long time

Neither the cartoon editor, Emma, or her associate Colin wrote back. When I talked to Liana, I asked her what day she finds out whether a cartoon has been bought.

"Is it still Friday?" I asked.

"Yes," she said. "But sometimes it comes in the middle of the night on Friday."

I was watching CNN at the gym in the afternoon and saw that Oklahoma is trying to ban all abortions, and it seems like they will be able to do it. It's all so horrifying, like we are living in a nightmare. How can religious extremists be in control of these states? It doesn't seem possible. When I came home I did a cartoon about it. A husband and wife are looking at their laptop screens and the wife says, "Oklahoma is trying to kill anyone who's ever thought about having an abortion." I doubt the *New Yorker* will go for it.

I texted Eve earlier and told her I submitted cartoons this week. She wrote:

What inspired you

I wrote back:

I have no idea

She asked what the cartoons were about and I told her one was inspired by a conversation with my friend Wendi, the mother of two kids Eve has known her whole life, and sent Eve the cartoon. A couple is in bed and the woman is on the phone saying, "We have COVID, then a wedding, then COVID, then a vacation, then COVID."

She wrote back:

I laughed
They should definitely publish that

The cartoon was one of Max's and Sarah's two favorites also, so maybe they will. But probably not.

MAY 20

The *New Yorker* bought the COVID cartoon. Around one thirty this afternoon, Emma sent an email with the subject heading:

OK

When the *New Yorker* buys a cartoon, it is called an OK for some reason. Then in the email she wrote:

Or rather, O.K.!!!!!!! So glad to have you back in the mix.

And she included the rough of the COVID cartoon. It's all very strange, because when I stopped doing cartoons, it felt very right. And earlier this week, when I started doing them again, it felt just as right.

I had my *Gilligan's Island* meeting at 3:45 p.m. It was short, but it seems like we are all planning to go forward. I told the two members of the family and their agent that I would generate some pages detailing the characters, stories, themes, and give it to Andrew Singer next week.

Earlier in the day, I was making chicken salad. As I took the bones out of the chicken, I remembered making a wish on the wishbone of the chicken when I was a kid. One of the biggest ways my life is different from my children's lives is the wishbone. They have absolutely no idea what a wishbone is, whereas I was always very aware of a wishbone and the supposed power it had.

You took one end of the wishbone, and someone else took the other end, and you both made wishes. Then you would pull and it would break apart. The wish of the person who got the bigger part would come true and the other's wouldn't.

It wasn't as if I actually believed that your wish could come true, but at the same time I always felt compelled to make a wish on the wishbone and would be sad if I lost.

I had two older brothers, and it seemed like they got their wishes more than I did. When I was young, I think they might have put their thumbs on the top of the wishbone, which almost guarantees that you win. But once I was aware of that, I made sure they never did that again.

The thing I think is most interesting about making a wish is that it clarifies what you want. I've surprised myself when facing the moment of making a wish.

Oh, that's what I want the most, I discover in that moment.

If I had a wishbone today and I had to wish for which television show to happen, the Glenn project or *Gilligan's Island*, I would actually vote for *Gilligan's*. I like Andrew, and in this moment, it seems like it would be fun to work on something so silly and fun, and so separate from the real world, which is awful.

MAY 21

I worked on my pages for *Gilligan's Island* today. I had thought it would be easy and relaxing, but it was actually quite draining, and stressful. I am tired of generating ideas and not getting paid. I just want to earn some money for my ideas.

I am starting to worry about money, so it is looking more and more likely I will take a job on *Life & Beth* if they want to hire me.

"How honest can I be with them?" I asked Kate today, about my *Life & Beth* meeting next week. "I would love to say that I have problems with the parts with the friends, and the Schlomo character is anti-Semitic."

She didn't answer, which of course is an answer.

"I guess if I want the job, I can't be honest," I said. And I guess I basically knew that before asking the question.

In general, it was a stressful day, mostly because I can't stop thinking about all these things we need to take care of before we move.

A worker from an appliance place came to look at our mysteriously beeping refrigerator today. He was very aggressive, and I
thought I would lose my mind talking to him, but mercifully he
left quickly and we defrosted the refrigerator and hopefully it is
fixed now.

Later in the day, I was driving and an off-the-grid person wandered through traffic, causing everyone to stop. This never used to
happen, but now it often happens. I wonder if the off-the-grid
people know this used to not happen. I wish I could ask them.

MAY 22

I worked on my *Gilligan's Island* pages all morning, then sent them
to Andrew Singer. Twenty minutes later, he wrote back:

> It's great. Mind if I send to Darren?

Darren is the agent representing the estate. I wrote back:

> Not at all
>
> But then are we going to get "creative thoughts"
> from the estate?

Andrew responded:

> If we do we may have to bolt

And then he sent it to Darren. I would be sad to bolt, at
this point. I definitely want *Gilligan's Island* to happen. As I
think about the world, I continue to have discomfort about how

"pretend" the world of the Glenn/Pete project is. It seems much more honest to do a daffy insane fantastical project like *Gilligan's Island*.

Also, when I think about the Glenn/Pete project, I get a pain in my chest. I know how unfun it is going to be.

MAY 23

It's 6:33 p.m. It's been a very Silent Monday. I worked on cartoons most of the day then made broccoli soup. Maybe I will email Andrew now to see if Darren responded to him.

MAY 24

Andrew texted back after I went to sleep:

Not yet other than to say he got it

I wrote back:

Tough Cookie

It has been a Silent Tuesday, which is not fun after a Silent Monday. I am waiting to hear about the counteroffers on the Glenn/Pete show, and Darren's response or perhaps the estate's response to my notes on *Gilligan's Island*.

I worked on cartoons again today and did various banking things, which took hours upon hours. I closed one bank account over the telephone, and one in person. Both experiences were like being in a different world, one I really didn't want to be in.

I took a walk in the afternoon with my friend Max. He asked me when my *Life & Beth* meeting was.

"June second," I said.

"Is it with Amy?" he asked.

"No, two guys," I said. "Kevin Kane and someone. Is he a writer?"

"No," Max said. "He's a producer and an actor on it. He plays her ex-boyfriend."

"Oh," I said. "And he directs some episodes, I think."

"Would you be the showrunner?" he asked.

"I have no idea," I said.

When I thought about having to have the meeting, I wanted to rest my head on Max's shoulder.

MAY 25

It's 1:30 p.m. I texted Max Barbakow five hours ago to see if he wanted to have lunch sometime and he hasn't responded. Now, of course, I am sure he has quit the project and doesn't know how to tell me.

I'm very unsettled today, as you can see. There is still no word from Showtime or Netflix. I emailed Dave and Patti, my lawyers, to see if they responded. Dave immediately wrote back that they haven't heard a word yet.

Part of the reason I am unsettled is that there was an extremely deadly mass shooting in Texas yesterday. Nineteen kids and two adults were killed. It happens every day, but somehow the numbers of this one are so shocking.

On the way to school, I told Henry I was having a hard time understanding how a person could walk into an elementary school and do this.

"Somehow it's easier for me to wrap my brain around it if it's just a public place. Not somewhere with little children," I said.

"I understand it," he said.

"What do you mean?" I said, unnerved.

"They want to do the worst possible thing," he said.

"Really?" I said.

"Yes," he said, with absolute certainty. I wonder if he is right.

MAY 26

I am still unsettled today. This shooting has undone me. I know these shootings happen every day and I usually just go about my day. But today, it is as if I am upset about every single one of these shootings for the last twenty years. My heart is so heavy when I think about it.

Still silence from everyone regarding the Glenn/Pete project and *Gilligan's Island*. I feel strange about even thinking about these projects while this shooting happened so recently. I am embarrassed I even sent the email to my lawyers yesterday and asked Max Barbakow to have lunch.

Max did finally text back. We plan to have lunch next week. He also wrote:

Feeling like we'll be at showtime yeah?
How are you feeling?

I wrote back:

My feelings about everything are complicated
I might be a complicated person

We can touch on it when we see each other

I like Max. I'm glad he didn't drop out of the project. Yet. This is what it is like to be me. I guess I should work on trusting that things can happen.

MAY 27

I just got off the phone. I was talking to my friend Gary about the shooting.

"I've been in a funk for the last two days," he said.

"Yeah," I said. "We all have."

We then talked about how awful it is, how nothing is ever going to change, and it is just going to happen over and over and over again.

Each day this week, as more information has come out, it has gotten worse and worse. I cried on and off about it yesterday. So far today, there have been no tears, but I just feel sad.

Henry has the day off, so we are going to have lunch. Then I am taking him to see the sculpture garden. I really need it this week.

MAY 28

It's a three-day weekend, after a week of silence regarding the Glenn/Pete project and *Gilligan's Island*. It is highly unlikely that I will hear anything on Tuesday, so the silence feels like it has descended for a while.

I'm still thinking and talking about the shooting. I was doing my morning pages and found myself writing that tragedies are part of life, sadness is part of life, unbearable losses are part of life. Life is perfect because it is what is. And what it is, is perfect. Just existing is perfect. It comforted me as I wrote it.

But as the day went on, it was hard to stay with the comfort of these thoughts.

MAY 29

In my pages this morning, I wrote:

> I want to be the person I used to be which
> hopefully I still am

If this journal ever gets optioned as a musical, this should be the eleven o'clock number, not that I really ever understood what an eleven o'clock number was. Maybe it should be the song that ends act one—that I understand.

It's just been such a dark week in the world, especially in this country.

MAY 30

I have been trying to do a cartoon about a hamburger who wants to feel complete instead of just waiting for someone to put tomato, lettuce, and ketchup on top of it. It is not funny, it doesn't make sense, and I feel I must be going mad with this feeling of just waiting for something—anything—to happen.

11:11 A.M.

Now it's a few hours later and I am a different person. Outside our house, a large bluebird just flew by me and there was something so dazzling about it that I thought I was the luckiest person in the world to see it. I could care less about my professional purgatory. I am just so grateful for all that I have. Sometimes I spend my whole day veering from thinking I am going mad to being filled with intense gratitude. And that may be its own form of madness.

MAY 31

Around noon today, I was in the kitchen and heard a familiar terrible sound. I opened the front door and saw a large bluish bird sitting near the front door, moving its head slightly, obviously in a daze from flying into the large glass window in the kitchen. I went inside, hoping it was merely in a daze because I am not in the mood to clean up a dead bird today. Of course I wondered if it was the bird I saw yesterday, and hoped it wasn't. It should always be sad when a bird dies and, in theory, just because you met the bird once yesterday, you shouldn't be sadder about it than if it were a bird you had never met. But I am and I am not sure why.

I waited twenty minutes then I brought out the recycling. The bird was in the same spot, still moving its head slightly. It almost looked like the bird was talking to itself. On my way back from recycling, the bird flew up in the air and landed a foot or two farther from the front door. I am now hoping that the bird is slowly getting into a steadier place and will fly away successfully.

6:21 P.M.
It's been a very silent Tuesday, as I expected.

Around one thirty I had to leave the house. I delicately opened the front door and looked outside. The blue bird was gone. I was somewhat relieved. But still scared the bird only flew a short way off and died elsewhere. I will never know, so I am trying to assume the bird is alive. When the bird looked like it was talking to itself, that definitely didn't seem possible.

Yesterday we visited a friend we have both known for a long time. And this friend just didn't seem as strong emotionally as he did when I first met him. It's been many, many years, and the decline has been somewhat steep.

Whenever people seem "crazier" than they used to be, I often think it is just because of the world, which seems to be less safe than it used to be. Or it's because the things that have happened to them personally have had a bad effect on them.

My friend Rachel disagrees. She said to me the other day that when someone seems worse than they used to be, it means they had something they needed to take care of and they didn't.

According to her way of thinking, we all have challenges we need to face. If we face them, we become more grounded and secure ultimately. If we don't, we just get more unhinged.

"Things just get bigger," she said. It made me reevaluate my point of view. I think she's right. Things do just get bigger.

JUNE 1

So. It's 4:31 p.m. and have not heard a word about the Glenn/Pete project or *Gilligan's Island*. I did hear from Rob's assistant Chloe. She confirmed my meeting with the two *Life & Beth* people tomorrow. I am dreading it. I have already forgotten most of the ten episodes I saw.

I met my friend Michelle at Erewhon Market and had lunch at one of the tables outside. We talked about a million things, but not *Life & Beth*.

I called her ten minutes after we said good-bye and went our separate ways.

"Do you miss me?" she said.

"No," I said. "I forgot to say my *Life & Beth* meeting is tomorrow. Do I have to take it?"

"Yes," she said. She didn't even take a pause before saying it. "I'm going to watch the first episode tonight."

"You really don't have to," I said.

So I am going now to read over synopses of the episodes that I saw weeks ago and now barely remember. Maybe I will also text Andrew about *Gilligan's Island*. I just wrote him:

Still nothing from the tough cookie?

4:50 P.M.

I read recaps of all the *Life & Beth* episodes. It wasn't a fond trip down memory lane. I then saw that Andrew texted back:

They sent me some thoughts from the family . . .
not necessarily in response to what you sent.
I'll forward.

I then read the email he forwarded. It was all about the spirit of the original and how that should remain in the new version. I agreed with all their thoughts.

I texted Andrew:

To me the thoughts are in synch with my pages
So do we go to Rovner

Rovner is the last name of Susan Rovner, the executive at Peacock who Andrew has talked with about the project.

Andrew answered:

I agree

I wrote back:

I have a meeting tomorrow at noon about working
on season 2 of Life & Beth

Can we sell this so I can cancel the meeting?

He answered:

Yes but not by then

When I think about the meeting, I get a pain in my chest and want to jump rope for twenty minutes. Maybe that's what I should do now.

JUNE 2

I woke up with the *Life & Beth* pain in my chest. Then I meditated and wrote my morning pages and found myself writing that maybe I could take the job and be happy. Is there a world where I could view the situation as an arranged marriage?

Maybe I could grow to love *Life & Beth*. Maybe this thing I don't want is the thing that I actually need and could benefit from. It's a real maybe, though.

2:10 P.M.

I had my meeting with the two producers Dan and Kevin. I am still not sure if either is actually a writer. Dan seemed to be more of a writer. And no one mentioned what my role would be on the show. But the meeting seemed to go well. At the end, Dan asked a question.

"Would it be all right if Amy called Lena and Jerry to ask about you?" he said.

"Sure," I said. I knew Amy was friends with Lena Dunham but didn't know she was friends with Jerry Seinfeld. I added, "*Seinfeld* was over twenty years ago, though, so I am not sure how relevant his information would be."

"She's very close with Jessica," Dan said, referring to Jerry's wife.

That makes sense because earlier in the conversation they said that Jerry and Jessica's daughter Sasha had just graduated college and would be part of the writers' room for *Life & Beth*.

I was so positive when I talked about the show with them that I have almost talked myself into liking it. I knew that could happen.

They said they were going to talk to other writers, then run names by Amy, who then would meet with those people.

"You should know something by the end of next week," Dan said.

"Take as much time as you want," I said. "I'm not going anywhere."

4:34 P.M.

Max Barbakow just texted to ask about finally having our lunch next Tuesday. I wrote back:

Great!

I was mildly resentful about having to put an exclamation point, which everyone expects you to, but there is no way around that.

I have been cleaning drawers and closets for the last hour or so, in preparation for relocating to New York on July 8.

There are so many things I need to take care of in the next five weeks, but I have to take it one day at a time or I will go mad.

After my meeting today, I wrote Ellyn, Laura, and Rob an email with the heading "Life & Beth/Gilligan":

> I just had my L&B meeting, seemed to go well, they're interviewing other people, etc. The dates for the show are starting end of July and going 16 weeks.

> I texted with Andrew Singer yesterday. The estate seems to have approved my pages, so now I believe the next step would be to pitch it to Peacock

Laura quickly wrote back:

> That's great—would be amazing to bypass the studio on this. We will follow

After a few hours, Ellyn wrote back:

> That really would be amazing.

> How did you feel about the vibe with the L&B team?

I answered:

> It was a very pleasant conversation
> I am not sure what else there is to say

Rob then wrote:

> If it were to materialize and we carved out the pilot would you be interested in working on it?

I answered:

I am definitely open to it
I would like to have more information

But since he was very up front that there are other contenders,
let's see if I even go to the next step and meet with Amy

In any case, that will inform my decision

No one chose to response to that.

JUNE 3

I have somehow spent hours trying to activate my new ATM card
for my checking account. Now I am starting to think the problem
is not the card, but me.

I asked Patti and Dave if there has still been silence from Showtime and Netflix. They said they haven't heard a word.

JUNE 4

I have not wanted to write much about my work life lately. I woke
up this morning in a bad mood about it all. Last night, Dave
emailed:

Both Showtime and Netflix are waiting on full counters
from Pete and Glenn before they counter back to everyone. Laura is pressing her colleagues to complete their
counters asap.

The slowness of Pete and Glenn's team infuriates me. I texted
Andrew Singer:

Now what?

He answered:

We go to Susan

Let's chat Monday to sort it out

I answered:

I can chat now

But he chose not to take me up on that.

The filtered water faucet in the kitchen is dripping. I called the plumbers yesterday but they didn't call me back. The roofers were here yesterday but can't guarantee that the roof is fixed. I don't understand why everything in this house is broken.

Plus, every single thing I read in the newspaper makes me tense.

I can't stop thinking about the dripping water faucet. It is as if it is a metaphor for everything in this world being horribly broken. So now every time I walk by the faucet and hear the drip, I get filled with upset and fear and anxiety.

JUNE 5

Today, I looked at the water leaking out of the faucet, and instead of seeing it as a metaphor for everything in the world being broken, all I saw was a drip. It's a very different way of looking at things.

Yesterday morning Henry and I went to visit my friends Winnie and Paul. We sat in their backyard and caught up, not having seen each other in a long time.

They mentioned they had watched all the episodes of *The Mary Tyler Moore Show* recently. It was one of my favorite shows as a kid and I know every episode by heart.

I think Mary's first apartment was one of the greatest television sets ever made. It may have been the first set that made me want to crawl into the television, and it may have created that feeling of peace I have whenever I am on actual television set, in my job as a writer and producer.

It was only a studio apartment, but it had a magical quality and didn't seem small at all. It seemed perfect. Especially compared to Rhoda's apartment upstairs, which was bleak.

Mary's apartment had a sweetness to it and was filled with hope, like she was. And since it was in Minneapolis, it was often snowing outside the enormous windows in the back wall. The snow was never depressing in any way. It was enormous fluffy snow and it only gave you a feeling of extra safeness that you were in Mary's apartment and not out there in the cold.

There have been so many terrible things happening in the world this week. I wonder if I can cultivate Mary's apartment's feeling of extra safeness that—at least for the moment—everyone in this house is okay.

JUNE 6

It's a Silent Monday, at least in terms of Glenn and Pete. Andrew Singer and I spoke this morning. He says we are all set to pitch *Gilligan's Island* to Peacock. He just has to run it by Universal, where Broadway Video has their deal.

"They may want to have a phone call with you first," he said. "Fine with me," I said.

I have continued to think about *The Mary Tyler Moore Show*. There were so few shows then, unlike now. There were just three networks who had shows from eight to eleven each night. And because of that, there was such a more communal feeling in terms of what people watched.

You just had three choices, and usually there was only one good choice. Every now and then there were two good choices, or no good choices.

I remember once a kid I knew said his family watched *Emergency* instead of *The Mary Tyler Moore Show*, and I found that to be shocking.

JUNE 7

I had lunch with Max Barbakow. He told me he had just spoken to his agent who said Glenn and Pete and Christian and all their reps are trying to figure out a way for the pilot to shoot in mid-August before Pete's other show starts shooting in September, as he will be unavailable for months and months.

"That's eight weeks or nine weeks from now," I said.

"Can we do that?" Max asked.

"I think so," I said.

I suggested my friend Ilene to be the line producer, and he was agreeable. And he suggested my friend Allison to be the casting person, and I of course was agreeable to that. They would be the first two people hired.

I asked him if Showtime was interested in us doing the show so quickly, and he wasn't sure. But after our lunch, I spoke to Laura at

CAA and she said Showtime does want the pilot to shoot sooner rather than later.

Glenn and Pete's counter went in yesterday, so if everyone's deal closes in the next week or two, this really could shoot in August.

JUNE 8

I spoke to Ilene last night. She can't work on the show, but she is going to think of other producers. I asked her about the timeline, and she said it was doable. But we would have to start hiring people a week or so from now, if we wanted to shoot end of August. I conveyed this to both Ellyn and Max.

It's hard to wrap my brain around us actually shooting this script. Even though we are so close, it still seems very far away from happening.

I have heard nothing from Andrew Singer about *Gilligan's Island* of course.

12:24 P.M.
Ellyn just texted:

> Bruce, Dan Powell wrote to us that Amy definitely
> wants to meet so his office will reach out to get
> that set.

Shit. I am hoping that the Glenn/Pete project really does shoot in August as that is the only thing that will get me out of this.

6:01 P.M.
After I got that text, I went into the kitchen and never came out of it. I made croutons, vegan Caesar dressing, vegan mayonnaise, chickpea tuna salad, and vegan cheesy broccoli rice for dinner.

JUNE 9

My meeting with Amy Schumer is set for Monday, June 13, at 9:40 a.m. I tried to get the 9:00 a.m. slot, but it was already taken. I asked Chloe, my agent's assistant, who my competition is.

Chloe said she would find out.

A few hours later, I received a text from Ellyn:

Bruce we're on with Patti and Dave re Showtime's response which came in last night.

Are you reachable in the next little bit if we call?

I said I was and we talked a few minutes later. The deal seems very close to being closed. They are going to try and get some of the numbers up a bit, but as far as I am concerned, this is it.

It's going to Showtime.

I reminded all that I would need to hire a line producer by next week to make the August dates work.

I then had lunch with Henry and then we picked up Eve at her friend Tabby's house. We dropped her off at the pediatrician for her to get her physical for Fieldston. While we were waiting outside, I saw there was a missed phone call from Gary.

I called him back excitedly. Michelle, Gary and his husband Brad, and Kate and I just had dinner two nights ago, so I knew if he was calling he must have a fun story to tell me.

"This is so exciting that you called," I said when he answered. "What's going on?"

"Brad has COVID," he said. At dinner we were joking because Brad had COVID thirty-one days ago.

"My doctor says you only get thirty days immunity with these new variants," Michelle said.

"So you're not safe anymore," someone else said, and we all laughed.

But her doctor apparently was right. We went home after the pediatrician and I immediately took a test. I looked at it after about four minutes and there was no line. I felt very confident that I would not be positive.

"There's no line," I said to Eve. She then walked over two minutes later and looked at the test.

"Uh-oh," she said.

I went over and looked at the test. There was now a faint line. I took a picture and texted it to Gary.

"I'm sorry," he said.

So it appears I have COVID. But maybe it won't be that bad. Andrew Singer just texted me about *Gilligan*:

> I spoke to the studio and I think they're going to
> be OK with us going directly to Peacock. Susan
> Rovner wants us to pitch it to Lisa Katz and Jeff
> Meyerson but she seemed enthusiastic

I just smiled as I typed:

> I am actually really excited about possibly doing
> Gilligan's Island.

JUNE 10

I had two negative at-home tests today, and went for a PCR. Gary emailed today that Brad's PCR was negative, so his rapid test was a false positive. But since I had a faint line (and Gary also got a faint line after one negative test), it seems strange that all three of us had false positives yesterday.

JUNE 11

The PCR results came during the night. I tested negative. So I officially only seem to have had COVID for a day. I haven't heard of this happening to anyone else.

I just got an invite to a screening of John and Kate's special for Peacock. I haven't been to a movie theater since we were in New Zealand during the pandemic. I am curious to see it but a little nervous about going to an event with a lot of people in a tight space, especially after my week of one-day COVID.

I am especially curious because Max wants to cast John and Kate as Glenn's son and daughter in the pilot. I agree and would love to see them in the parts. I think they would both do it, if it fits into their schedules. But both are already regulars on other shows, so that may be tricky for Showtime, who might want them to be in first position.

It's Saturday and I have had the most boring day. The highlight may have been the half hour I spent lying on the ground in the backyard. I have been doing it a few times a week. Today, I listened to the sounds from the other backyards and felt like I was a kid in New Jersey in the 1970s once again.

5:39 P.M.

Oh boy. I just read in the newspaper that Julee Cruise died. Suicide. I feel so sad. I hadn't thought about her in years and years. She sang a song that was in the first episode of *Twin Peaks* and then she released an album. I listened to that album maybe five hundred times. I played it over and over and over again. There was one summer where, at least in my memory, that was all I listened to. I was twenty-five and living in a tiny apartment in an alley behind Hayworth Avenue. There were two apartments next to each other above two garages in the alley. So the apartment was basically the size of a car.

That summer was so hot, although strangely not as hot as now. But I had no air-conditioning, so it seemed hotter. I remember one crazily hot day, I just listened to Julee Cruise again and again, and it was as if she got me through that hot day.

I'm listening to the album now as I type this. It makes me feel like I am once again living in that world, a world without people who believed in insane conspiracy theories and the conservative people in the House and the Senate were almost normal. I would literally give anything to go back to that day.

JUNE 12

I'm still listening to Julee Cruise. Tomorrow is my Amy Schumer meeting at 9:40 a.m. I am definitely going to take this job if I get it and nothing else is happening. It's a real odd and unexpected twist. I am determined to go with the flow at this exact moment.

I talked to Michelle. I think I sounded a bit mad.

"Waiting is hard for you," she said. I have always thought I moved at a different speed than the rest of the universe.

We then spoke about Julee Cruise and how she died.

"I think we are going to start to read about a lot more suicides in this time," I said.

"Yeah," she said.

At the farmers market this morning, I passed the man who sells honey who is always blaring some horrible music. Today, mercifully, he was playing "When You're in Love with a Beautiful Woman" by Dr. Hook. It's a disco song from my childhood.

"I haven't heard this in forty years," I said to the honey man with a big smile on my face. The song ended and he smiled at me and started it again from the beginning.

"It's the best song," I said and moved on.

JUNE 13

My meeting with Amy Schumer ended at 10:00 a.m. on the dot. It was exactly twenty minutes. I told her what I loved about the show and what I was interested in for season two, and she said I was hired.

"Great," I said. And then told her about the possibility that the Glenn-and-Pete show would happen and I might not be available. I don't know why I found myself agreeing to go on the show. I was just going with the flow, I guess.

I recently had this sensation that all things in the world were totally connected, and somehow I feel my saying I would do her show is connected to all things being connected.

JUNE 14

Kate Berlant texted an invite to a screening of her Peacock special with John on Saturday night. She added:

Talk the week of the 27th

I said I couldn't go to the screening, but said:

Yes, let's talk then!

Rob and Laura told me that Amy wants to hire me but has to run my name by the production company, which should take about a week. They reiterated that the dates might not work if the Glenn/Pete project shoots in August.

They went on to say that Pete is "on vacation" and Ayala can't confirm that he has signed off on the five days in August we are looking at for him to work.

JUNE 15

I called Christian today to check in. It is Wednesday, and Ilene said I would be in trouble if I didn't find a line producer by the end of this week.

Christian said he and Glenn really want this to shoot in August.

"This can't wait until 2023," he said. "Showtime is really excited about this show. They said this pilot would be their most expensive half hour ever shot."

"Hmm," I said. I was thinking that other than Glenn's and Pete's salaries, this shouldn't be that expensive a show.

"The deals are all close to being closed," he said. "All we are waiting on is for Pete to confirm the dates. He's on vacation and Ayala can't get in touch with him."

"I heard," I said. "Where is he on vacation?"

"I don't know," he said.

"Just look at Page Six," I said. "I'm sure it's there."

"Hold on," he said. "I'll check."

A few seconds later he said, "They're in Tahiti," referring to him and Kim Kardashian.

"When do they get back?"

"End of the month."

"Oh," I said.

"I told Glenn yesterday she has to contact him to get an answer and she is supposed to do that today or tomorrow."

When I got off the phone, I thought, this really looks like it's going to happen.

JUNE 16

Oh boy. I just got off the phone with Laura and Rob.

"I don't want to freak you out," Laura said. That's not a good beginning. "But we wanted to give you a heads-up about something."

Uh-oh, I thought. This really doesn't sound good.

"Ayala has been in touch with Pete, and she says he's overwhelmed," Rob said.

We talked for a while. Basically, Christian spoke to Ayala, who said Pete is not officially out, but it doesn't look good.

"If Ayala isn't being optimistic, then this really does seem to be over," I said.

They said that everybody including Showtime still wants to shoot in August, so that is good. Laura started pitching me other names to take Pete's place.

"It seems like Glenn has to be attracted to the actor," I said. "And I have no idea who she is or isn't attracted to. So there is no point in pitching me names."

We talked for a while longer, all saying that Pete dropping out might be for the best. Eve and Henry are going to be devastated, sadly.

JUNE 17

I just read that Will Forte is going to be in a new TV show for Netflix produced by the Obamas. It has been months and months since I was supposed to meet with him for my New Zealand idea. Evan Moore, the executive who I was developing it for, just ghosted me. In a perverse way, I am greatly looking forward to my next interaction with Evan Moore, whenever that will be.

It is one of the most depressing things in the world to me that the Obamas have chosen to become TV producers. When I think about it, I just want to cry.

I had a thought this morning that every person I come into

contact with is my teacher. My time with any person is an opportunity to learn something. Then I had a thought that everything that happens to me or that I observe is also my teacher. The faucet that has been dripping for almost two weeks and that will hopefully be fixed when the plumber comes for a second time on Monday has taught me to drink more water in a way that nothing else has. I put a glass under the faucet every time I walk by it to use up the dripping water. It's truly been life-changing. Or at least it feels that way.

Maybe the feeling of something being life-changing is all we need. It doesn't matter whether it actually is or not. Or rather, the feeling is what is life-changing.

I can't believe I am on page 199 of this book (which for some reason became page 228 when this book became an actual book) and I am just sitting here, waiting for Pete, on Friday, the last day I have to hire a line producer and make this actually happen in August. But actually, I can believe it. I am sitting here smiling about it in fact. It's perfect. This moment feels absolutely perfect.

Maybe I should call this book *Page 199*. And this could be the last page.

Because I am actually not waiting for Pete at all. I am just being. It took me 199 pages to get here. I hope I can stay just being forever, and it won't just be on page 199.

JUNE 18

Around noon yesterday, I thought, it's been a while since I've heard from Andrew Singer, so I went to go text him. I looked at the phone and saw our last exchange had been eight days ago. I sent him a text:

Now what are we waiting on?

He quickly texted back:

Me mostly. I've been in Vancouver dealing with a
giant cluster fuck on Schmigadoon

I'll get it scheduled today though

I then texted:

I can ask Laura and Rob to do it if that's
preferable

He answered:

Nope it's all good

I never heard back, so I guess he didn't get it scheduled yesterday
as he said he would. I really don't care, though. I'm just being.

JUNE 19

Kate and I went to a surprise birthday party for her agent yesterday.
Earlier in the week, we looked at the RSVPs and I saw that Amy
Israel, the Showtime executive, was going to be there.

We saw her seconds after we arrived. I stopped to talk to someone, and moments later I saw Kate talking to Amy. I walked up to
them and they were clearly talking about the Glenn/Pete project.

"It only took you two seconds to bring it up," I said, looking at Kate.

"It seemed natural," she said with a smile. "It was obviously on our minds."

"This is a social thing," I said.

"Okay, okay," Kate and Amy both said. I feel like there is a rule not to bring up business at a social event, but maybe I am wrong.

Hours later, Amy came up to me when I was alone. "I do want to say one thing," she said.

"Of course, say anything you want," I said. "I just didn't want you to talk about work if you didn't want to."

"I really hope this happens," she said.

"I assume it is happening," I said. "Isn't it?"

"Well, the deals have to close."

"Christian told me all the deals were close to closing."

We then talked about Pete for a while and then Amy looked at me a little nervously.

"If we want to make these dates in August," she said, "we are really on the edge."

"I know," I said. "But we can still make the dates. We are just on the edge."

"I know," she said. "I'm just really nervous."

"I'm not," I said. "I know we are on the edge, but as I always tell Max Barbakow, everything is unfolding in a divine and perfect order. We can make the dates."

At one point during the party, I looked around and saw Casey Bloys, who is the head person at HBO. I have no idea what his title is. I basically have no idea what anyone's title is. I know Casey and waved hello. I wanted to go up to him and tell him that I saw him at my friend Willie's memorial service and how nice it was to see him there. Willie would have really appreciated it. Casey being there showed that Willie was valued and that was a kind act. To me, it shows that Casey has a good heart.

Sadly, I didn't go up to Casey, because just like I couldn't speak at Willie's memorial. I felt I would fall into a million pieces if I tried to say this out loud, and I didn't want to fall into a million pieces at this party.

This morning I decided to send Amy Israel an email. It read:

Great to see you last night

I know we are on the edge but I also know it's all going to work out

I am thrilled to be doing this one with you

She didn't write back.

Today is Father's Day. Some days I can't believe how lucky I am to be a father and this day is certainly one of them. We did nothing today and I had the greatest day of my life.

JUNE 20

It's the end of day. Amy Israel still hasn't written back. But that might not indicate anything. I nervously checked my phone all morning while I did things out in the world. Then when I saw Kate in the afternoon and asked if she'd heard anything about a work thing, she said, "They all have off."

"What?" I said.

"It's Juneteenth," she said.

But it was Juneteenth yesterday, I thought. So here we are. It is a nationally sanctioned Silent Monday.

A few weeks ago, a friend of mine told me his agent was traveling.

"He's always traveling," my friend said. "And I know I'm always traveling. But I don't travel like this. He is constantly on vacation."

"They love vacations," I said. And, relatedly, they love days off.

JUNE 21

Silent Tuesday. It's five o'clock and no one has said a word about anything. I just did cartoons, took Eve to Torrance for a volleyball clinic, cleaned, then did more cartoons.

Periodically I felt like I was going mad, then recalibrated and was okay. I had a low point in Torrance while I was driving on what seemed to be the ugliest street in the world for what started to feel like hours. I just moaned periodically, then felt a little better once I got on the highway. There was terrible traffic on the 405, but it was still better than Torrance.

JUNE 22

Well, Pete is officially out. Ellyn, Rob, and Laura called around noon.

"Pete doesn't want to shoot this in 2022," one of them said. "And Glenn doesn't want to shoot this in 2023."

There was a lot of discussion about what Showtime will want.

The hope is that they are open to another actor and we still shoot this end of August, or more realistically the beginning of September.

I am trying to figure out how I feel and the only thing I can really be sure about is: I don't want to go on *Life & Beth*, which is looking more and more likely.

JUNE 23

I woke up this morning and thought, This book should have ended on page 199. Maybe it still will.

JUNE 24

I never heard a word from anyone yesterday. I texted Max Barbakow:

> I haven't heard anything new
> Have you?
> It's more fun to hear from you than them

He texted back:

> No but Glenn wants to talk in the next hour so I'll
> try her and then you

I said:

> Sounds good

An hour passed and I didn't hear anything from him. I thought about texting him, but I didn't. Finally he texted:

> Didn't get her

It is 7:44 a.m. and I am already having such a strange day. I went to the *New York Times* and was stunned by the headline at the top of the page: "Supreme Court Overturns Roe v. Wade."

Of course, like everyone, I knew this was most likely coming. But it is still so shocking and hard to wrap your brain around. What world has this become? How are we all supposed to go about our day?

Minutes later, the most beautiful and familiar music came on the classical music radio station KUSC. I looked at the title. It turned out to again be "Happiness Does Not Wait" by Ólafur Arnalds. It's a reminder that beauty coexists with ugliness. Intense ugliness.

10:53 A.M.

I feel very shaky. I went to the gym, and found myself constantly looking at my phone to check my email. Oddly, it wasn't for any information about the Glenn project. It was almost like I wanted to get an email that would magically take me out of this reality where religious extremists are on the Supreme Court and are making decisions unconnected to law.

It reminded me of something that happened over twenty years ago. Kate and I had been dating for a few months when her aunt died. I flew with her to go to the funeral somewhere in Westchester County in New York. I met her parents and, of course, the rest of her family that day.

After the funeral we went to her aunt's house. At one point, I went to the bathroom. In the hall, I saw her widowed uncle leave the main room where all the guests were and go off into a small room by himself. I watched him sit down at his computer and heard him sign into AOL mail.

How can he be checking his email on the day of his wife's funeral, I thought. Then I decided it was just a way to not be in his reality. That was me this morning. I guess it's how we all are a lot of the time.

JUNE 25

I wandered through my day yesterday in a fog. I texted Rob, Laura, and Ellyn in the middle of the day:

First I would like to acknowledge it's a creepy day

Second is there any update

Ellyn wrote back:

It's awful

Laura wrote:

It is. And no update unfortunately

Ellyn wrote:

We were just texting . . . no news re Glenn

I asked:

What does Showtime know?

Laura answered:

Nothing

Glenn wanted to try to reach out to Pete again
before we told Showtime

I said:

Oh

I didn't know that

So should I tell Max that? Or will he already know

Laura responded:

I think Glenn wanted to hear from Pete directly
he's out versus through the grapevine of agents

I think it's more of a courtesy than a convincing
him to change his mind

I said:

Ok

But what doesn't add up is not telling Showtime

That can only mean she wants to convince

There was silence on the chain. That somehow stopped the conversation. Then a little while later, Ellyn wrote:

We need to tell Showtime something before the
end of the week

It was Friday afternoon when she wrote that, so I wrote:

This is the end of the week

After a while, Laura texted:

From Glenn's agent: She hasn't heard back from
him. But if she doesn't hear back over the weekend
I will get back into it with her and tell her we've
done all we can do and need to keep it moving.

I talked to Max a little later. He, of course, had all the information already.

"My agent said Glenn wants to make one last play to get him to do it," he said.

"I assumed," I said. "My agent said she wasn't going to try to convince him, but that didn't make sense to me."

JUNE 26

It is 11:03 a.m. and it has already been a three-trips-to–Vicente Foods day.

JUNE 27

Kate and I were home last night when she received this email from her agent:

Subject: Traveling / Holiday

Hi Friend.

With the town and offices closing down Friday July 1st through July 8th for the holiday, I wanted to let you know I will be skipping town a few days early on Wednesday June 29th to head overseas for a holiday. If there is anything pressing/time sensitive over this time—it will be easiest to reach me on email (rather than text or phone). Apologies if it takes a beat with time change—and if it is something that can wait until I return to the office on Monday July 11th—I will be refreshed and recharged.

*Also, [his assistant's name] will be reachable and then when we close—7/1–7/8 [his assistant's email address]

Thanks everyone.

I had no idea the town was closed then. That doesn't normally happen. Also, what I don't understand is, if the town is closed, why do the assistants have to work?

It has been ten days since Andrew Singer said he was going to set the *Gilligan* meeting with Peacock. I just texted him:

Did Gilligan die?

He wrote back almost immediately:

No but universal wants to make the rights deal
with the estate before we pitch. Their point is we
would have to do it after anyway so it doesn't
actually hold the project up. Rovner worried the
estate will have unreasonable expectations and
if we wait till after the sale they'll have too much
leverage

Then he added:

I just heard this on Friday which is why I hadn't
talk to her yet. Was planning to call you this
morning.

Which is why I hadn't told you her Which is why I
hadn't told you yet God this dictation feature!

I wrote back:

Ok

Although I don't understand the leverage part

If they ask for too much, why couldn't we just say
eh and walk away

Andrew answered:

I can make that point

I was confused so I wrote:

Seems odd that I would be only person to think this

They must know something I don't

Andrew said:

They just wouldn't want to put you in the position
of having sold a show and then not being able to
close the underlying rights

I answered:

Fine with me to do that

It happened with the topical show at Sony for Hulu
basically

As you may remember

I was referring to something that happened when I was on my
deal at Sony a few years ago. I had lunch with the person running
Hulu at the time and sold him an idea for a topical show during
our lunch. Then I told Sony I sold a show, and asked Andrew

Singer to be involved. I started fleshing the idea out and generating pages that Andrew gave notes on, but we never actually moved forward because Sony and Hulu couldn't make a deal. I think it was because Sony felt there would be no international interest in a show that was topical, so it didn't make sense financially.

It is 9:38 a.m. It feels like I am going to find out this Glenn project has totally fallen apart today.

3:14 P.M.

Around noon, John Early texted:

Hi Bruce! Comin' up for air.

Maybe we can talk some time early next week?

In our last texting communication, Kate had asked:

Talk the week of the 27th?

Which obviously would have been this week. It feels like they will keep pushing, which is fine with me. I have lost my steam with John and Kate. Truthfully, I watched their Peacock special the other night, and while there is a lot that is interesting about it, I did begin to wonder if I was the right match for them.

An hour later, I got a text from Rob at CAA:

Just fyi—we spoke to Glenn's agent this morning.
Glenn hasn't heard from Pete still so he's asking
her if we can now tell showtime today that he's out

I am assuming Glenn won't answer his question today.

JUNE 28

A lot happened yesterday after I assumed Glenn wouldn't answer her agent's question. Let me see if I can get it all down right.

Around four o'clock, Max Barbakow texted me:

Talked to Glenn

She still hasn't heard from Pete

I answered:

I heard this am Let's hear all

He wrote:

Wanted to set a zoom for tomorrow to all touch base and decide what to tell showtime

I thought, Why do we have to meet? We can just tell them the truth. But I didn't feel like having a back-and-forth, so I simply wrote:

Ok

Forty-five minutes later, I was on the phone with my friends Sarah and Max, giving them an update.

"I don't know why he wants to meet," I said.

"He always wants to meet," Max said. Then a text came in from Max Barbakow, which I then read to them:

I just talked to my rep who I guess has connected

with everybody's—she says only move is to tell
Showtime Pete has ghosted, which I think is right.
You okay with everybodys reps calling Showtime?
Don't think we need to necessarily zoom about it.
At this point the dude has vanished
Just texted Glenn this too

I wrote back:

Perfect
Seems right to me

A little later Ellyn, Rob, and Laura started texting me. Laura said she would contact Jessie at Showtime, since Amy Israel is on vacation. Later, she texted:

Spoke to Jessie. She's bummed but said she's
going to discuss with team. Nothing definitive yet.

We ate dinner outside at the Ping-Pong table, as a friend of Eve's exposed her to COVID.

I gave everyone an update about the project, and we started talking about other actors for Pete's part.

"I had an idea the other night when I was awake and couldn't go back to sleep," Kate said. She looked at me. "Bo Burnham."

"I love it," I said. "I absolutely love it.

Years ago, CAA asked me if I would supervise a pilot Bo Burnham wrote (that ultimately went to Showtime, I think). I really loved the script but didn't think I wanted to supervise the show, as it was a little too dark for my personal taste. But my agent at the time wanted us to get a cup of coffee, so I agreed to that.

I asked him to meet me at the restaurant next to where Henry and Eve practiced martial arts so I could drop them off, meet with him, then pick them up.

I loved the hour I spent with him and we exchanged email addresses, so I could actually reach out to him directly, if he has the same address.

In a way, I think he is better than Pete. He definitely seems smarter. And I like that he has a daffiness like Pete.

"Why did you wait days to tell me?" I asked Kate.

"Sometimes you don't want to hear my ideas," she said, which is, sadly for her, very true.

After dinner, I texted Max Barbakow:

Kate had an idea I love

Then in invisible ink, I wrote:

Bo Burnham

I went to sleep without hearing back from Max. In the middle of the night, I woke up and read his response:

Love him but do you buy him as an ex-con

I went back to sleep. When I woke up in the morning, I answered him:

I'm hoping to a little bit buy it And that might be
the right amount

A half hour later, Max answered:

Worth exploring.

Which sounds like he is not that excited by Bo.

After I sent Max the text, I sat down to meditate. A minute or two later, I heard a text come in. I reached for my phone and saw it was a message from Laura:

> Hi everyone—I saw Jessie Dicovitsky last night. It
> sounds like she wants to try to keep this project
> together, and said if so, she'd definitely need
> CAA's help on casting. I mentioned Sebastian Stan
> as an idea, and she said that's someone she had
> been thinking of too, which feels like a positive
> sign. She still needs to discuss recasting with rest
> of team. Amy's on vacation.

I immediately wrote back:

> I love a 6:28 AM text

And for the next twenty minutes or so, as I meditated, I occasionally paused to text with that chain as messages came in. It was a fun way to meditate, since it is usually just me and my breath, day in and day out.

I suggested Bo Burnham and Rob said he loves him, but thinks Bo wants to focus on writing and directing. That wasn't very encouraging. Other names they mentioned were Jason Bateman, Jon Hamm, Miles Teller, and Eddie Redmayne. I barely know who the last two are, but none are that interesting to me. It was decided they would generate a list for me and Max, then we would shorten it and give it to Glenn.

JUNE 29

I woke up today in disbelief that this Glenn project has really started to go backward. Two weeks ago we had Pete and now we have no one.

Also, I forgot to give the update on *Life & Beth* from yesterday. I spoke to Ellyn and told her it had been weeks since I had heard whether I got approved by Endeavor Content, the company producing *Life & Beth*.

"I thought it was whether the offer got approved," she said.

"No," I said. Then went back to see what I had written about it. I sent her a screenshot that "my name" had to get approved by Endeavor Content. That is definitely not an offer.

She then texted Rob and Laura and sent me a screenshot of their texts later in the day. Ellyn kept asking them if my offer is getting approved, even though she knows it is my name that needs to be approved. Rob and Laura texted that my name has supposedly been approved by Endeavor Content. But now it seems my name is waiting approval by Hulu. It feels like after Hulu approves it, or if Hulu approves it, then my name will be sent to God to see if God approves it.

I heard nothing from anyone about anything today. When I walked out of the house at noon, I saw what appeared to be a dead lizard a foot from the front door. I just came home five hours later and the lizard is still there, so now I have to clean the dead lizard up. It's strange because the lizard looks like itself, just dead. It is as if a lizard came to our doorstep to die of old age.

JUNE 30

I was exhausted last night, mostly lying on the couch, then went to bed and slept for nine hours. I woke up and then went back to the couch and slept a little more. I think this book is actually turning into my suicide note.

10:38 A.M.

Laura just texted:

> Spoke to Netflix. Sounds like they were concerned about Pete's fee anyway, so this might be welcome news. Fingers crossed

So, strangely, maybe this will end up at Netflix.

12:05 P.M.

I was just in the car with Eve and showed her the text, since she prefers the show be at Netflix over Showtime.

"How long has this whole thing been going on?" she asked.

"I first met with Glenn last August," I said. "So almost a year."

"You should get a new career," she said.

JULY 1

It's Friday before the long weekend or the long week that the town is taking off according to Kate's agent, so of course I did not hear anything today. Supposedly people were working until lunchtime, but it feels like just the assistants were.

It is now one week until we move to New York, which is very anxiety inducing. I am hoping at some point to feel normal again, if I ever did feel normal.

Currently, it is five o'clock and Henry and I are both in the living room, typing on our laptops. He is furiously tapping away, which could agitate me at other times, but in this moment, it is the most soothing sound I can think of to hear.

"Do you want to play Ping-Pong now?" he just said.

I looked at him strangely, then told him to look at my laptop. Then I laughed. He walked over and looked at my screen, and read the last few paragraphs. He laughed.

I then said, "Yes."

JULY 2

I texted Max Barbakow midday yesterday, asking if he received the drawing I put in the mail to him on Monday. Last night he texted back that he hadn't, but was away so maybe it will have arrived by the time he gets back Monday.

He then started texting me ideas to replace Pete, a lot of whom I am unfamiliar with, so I said I would look at clips of them. At one point he suggested Jake Johnson. I wrote back:

I love him So much

Loved working with him

Max he's fun

I told Kate, and she said, "You mean Jake Lacy."

"Right," I said. Part of me knew it even as I was texting. It was slowly dawning on me just as Kate told me. So I texted back:

Wait

I was thinking of Jake Lacy But I also like Jake
Johnson

He answered:

Jake Lacy would be fantastic!

I ran it by my friends Max and Sarah. Max was mildly positive, but Sarah still feels Bo Burnham would be better.

It's been a strange week. It is now seven days since *Roe v. Wade* was overturned, then day after day the creepy religious freaks on the Supreme Court did other creepy things. I am not sure this is the exact definition, but my definition of creepy religious freak is someone who wants to impose their own personal religious beliefs onto other people. It is especially creepy to me when this person is a lawyer who should understand the separation of church and state. I keep hoping this is the moment where the one step back ends, and the next two steps forward begins. But it doesn't quite feel that way.

I just did a cartoon of two women talking and one is saying "Anna Wintour says creepy religious extremists are having a moment." I wanted to write "freaks" but felt the *New Yorker* would never buy it if I did. They probably won't buy it anyway. I didn't sell any cartoons this week, and I thought the group of eleven I sent them was very strong. There is no art meeting for the next two weeks, so let's see if they buy this one at the next art meeting in mid-July.

JULY 3

A few days ago I had a thought about all the things that keep breaking in this house. It is like the house is tired and just wants a break from us. When we move to New York, our neighbor Chris is going to watch over the house and use it as his office for a few hours a day. That seems like what the house needs for a while.

The four of us are just too much for it. I think the pandemic pushed a lot of the houses to the brink.

I had a thought about today. What if I just moved through the day, looking for something to be grateful for no matter what situation I was in? What would it look like to be annoyed or stressed or worried, but at the same time, also appreciative of an object that is in my sight, or just appreciative of just my breath in that moment? I know I am going to fail at this, but I want to give it a shot and see what happens.

JULY 4

I ended last night alone in the backyard, not wanting to be with anyone in the house. Earlier in the day, the four of us were in the car on the way to my friend Michelle's house. Henry and Eve got into an argument.

"Don't give me that look," he said.

"I didn't give you a look," she said.

"You looked at me annoyed," he said.

"I wasn't annoyed," she said.

"Yes you were!"

"Don't tell me how I feel," she said. "I tell people how I feel. I'm not like Dad."

I was very upset, and Eve and I got into a fight that lasted about thirty seconds, but we were both very upset. Eve said maybe she should have stayed at her boarding school. She looked at me with what seemed to be total hatred.

"You're right," I said, giving her back the look I felt she was giving me, childishly wanting to retaliate. "Maybe you should have."

All four of us then sat in silence.

Five minutes later, I had to run out of the car to pick up something. When I came back, Eve was crying.

"What did I miss?" I said.

Kate said it wasn't the best time to talk about it. I then calmly told Eve I was sorry I had spoken back to her with anger. I was just matching the anger she was giving me. But she was clearly still upset. So we all went to my friend Michelle's for a few hours and everyone acted normal.

A few hours later, when we were home, Kate and I got into a fight about my fight with Eve. Eve had said something in the two minutes the three of them were alone in the car that Kate wouldn't share. But as we discussed it, Kate indicated that something in my behavior with Eve was affecting Eve's relationship with me. It was something I also do with Kate and was affecting our relationship.

"Did Henry indicate it is affecting his relationship with me?"

"No," she said. "He just wanted the conversation to be over."

"So you think it is affecting my relationship with him?"

"Maybe," she said in a way that indicated she did feel that way.

She said she was not going to tell me what Eve said and what this thing was that I do. She wanted to wait until she figured out the best way to have the conversation with me.

"Can't we just table it for a few days?" she asked.

"It's easy for you to table it because you are not the one everyone has a problem with," I said. It took her a while to understand that, but finally she did.

"I'm very upset," I said. But there was nothing more really to say.

"It's just a little thing," she said.

"It doesn't feel like a little thing by the way you are talking about it," I said.

"But it is little," she said.

"But if it were really little, it would feel little in your tone of voice," I said. We fought about that for a while, then there was really no more to say.

I was very quiet during dinner, and then after dinner, I found myself not comfortable in the house, so I went outside.

Something in the conversation with Kate made me feel I didn't know how to make any of them feel loved.

If there is one thing you need to do with your children and your partner, it is to make them feel loved.

So there I sat at a table by myself, looking at the three of them inside the house, wondering if it would be better if the three of them didn't have to live with me.

Maybe I'm just not good at having a family, I thought. It was an experiment that didn't work out. The kids seemed to have turned out okay, but maybe that was in spite of me, which often happens. I don't know what is wrong with my brain, but sometimes I can go to the darkest possible place in it at lightning speed.

All night, there had been extremely loud music coming from a neighbor's party. Normally, I would be highly annoyed and in an agitated state. But last night, in the backyard, I just sat there and enjoyed the music. Song after song, I just let it wash over me. I gave in to the neighbor's loud music, and it was so much nicer than fighting it.

JULY 5

I was sad most of yesterday. I talked to Kate about it. She agreed that while she does feel loved, she would like to feel more loved. And that is probably true of the kids.

"I can try to do better," I said. "And will. But this is me giving a hundred twenty percent right now."

She said that all four of us should go to family counseling, but I told her that if the kids didn't want to go, which they wouldn't, then that didn't feel right to me. So we agreed that just she and I would go, at least at first.

I had to act normal and we had nothing to do, so I suggested we go all go to Canter's Delicatessen, which Henry had read about and wanted to see. We went there and I was happy to return to the neighborhood I had lived in when I first moved to Los Angeles. I spent years and years and years going to Canter's. We ordered food to go as we are still mostly not eating inside restaurants. I stood outside and looked around. It all looks so different from how it did thirty years ago. It looks worse, of course. The kids came out and joined me.

"You see that?" I said, pointing to a corner up the street. "That's the corner where Amy and I got mugged."

I had told them the story about how one night my friend Amy and I were parking and getting out of my car when suddenly a car pulled up. A man got out of the car, pointed a gun at us, looked at Amy, and said, "Give me your purse."

Amy froze. She just stood there, not making a move. "Give me your purse," he said again.

She didn't make a move.

"Give him your purse! Give him your purse!" I said, not wanting to get shot.

She finally made a move. She dropped her purse at her feet. If the man wanted it, he was going to have to walk over to us to get it.

The man looked at her angrily, then got back in the car, and the driver peeled out. Amy had miraculously intuited that he wasn't going to take the time to come get her purse.

We must have called the police, although this was before cell phones, so I have no memory of how we notified the police. Then we went to eat at Damiano's Mr. Pizza across the street from Canter's.

Now, thirty years later, I stood outside Cantor's, looking at what had been Damiano's Mr. Pizza.

I remember that when Amy and I finally got to Damiano's Mr. Pizza and ate our pizza, we laughed hysterically about our night, giddy beyond giddy. I think our laughter came from the high of the feeling of being alive. Is it possible to get that high without having someone point a gun at you an hour earlier? I wonder.

JULY 6

I talked to my friend Rachel yesterday and everything shifted. I feel fifty pounds lighter than I did yesterday. She made me understand that I could remove judgment from any of my interactions with Kate, Henry, and Eve, and that one change changed everything. I came home after talking to her and happily implemented what we talked about. I literally feel like a different person, as if my cells actually changed.

I think the reason I feel so much lighter is that when I stopped judging them, I magically stopped judging myself. It feels like no one ever told me that. It is the most basic thing, but it is life-changing. I wonder if everyone knows this except me. Maybe I heard someone say it once, or I read it somewhere, but it took over half a century for me to really learn it.

Earlier in the day, I had to go to my storage facility on Pico. It is my least favorite place on earth. There are always off-the-grid people in the dark halls, and I am sure that one could become violent at any second. I was sweating with fear as I tried to open the lock on my door. Finally, I did it and hurriedly put some boxes in, then locked it, and scurried down the hall. When I reached my car, I took a deep breath. I was a little giddy, like I was with Amy at Damiano's Mr. Pizza.

I got in my car and went to see Rachel. On the drive, I suddenly felt this enormous release.

I don't have to do any of this, I thought to myself. I was referring to John and Kate (who haven't reached out, although they are supposedly going to reach out this week), Glenn, *Gilligan's, Life &*

Beth (which still seems to be running my name past Hulu, although I think the writers' room should have started weeks ago), none of it. I haven't gotten paid for anything in over a year and I haven't had any fun. The closest thing to fun is that I have a fondness for Max Barbakow, and his texts always bring a smile to my face.

But when I think about only doing cartoons and just living my life and, strangely, making dinner for Kate, Henry, and Eve, that seems like enough in this moment. So this book is not a suicide note at all. It has an unexpected happy ending. It feels amazing to not need or want anything other than what I have. It might be the greatest feeling.

In forty-eight hours, we go to New York to begin our lives there. I have been racing around all morning doing things I should have done before forty-eight hours before we are leaving.

A few days ago, I thought to myself, I bet this book is going to end in about twenty or thirty pages. So when I sat down to write today, I had no idea that this book was ending today.

But it feels like it just did.

Back in January, when I had the dream and wanted to tell Glenn and Max that I wanted this to be a profound experience, I thought I was talking about shooting the television show. But it turns out that not shooting the television show was a profound experience, at least it was for me. So that's why the book ended. I wanted this to be a profound experience and I got it. This is the end of the book. Except for not really.

There's an afterword.

AFTERWORD

Two days later, we landed in Newark and I checked my texts. There was one from Rob:

Hey Bruce-we just tried you but your phone
went straight to VM. Ripping the band-aid off:
Showtime doesn't want to move forward without
Pete. They are happy to pick it back up if Pete
wants to do it come Spring, but we wanted to
discuss your appetite given what a roller coaster
this had been (we'd need to do the same with
everyone else involved and we have not been able
to reach Christian) As discussed, we will discuss
transitioning this to a blind with Amy directly since
we know how much she loves you and your voice.
We are so sorry and frustrated and around to talk
if you'd like

I wrote back:

Just landed in NYC
Its not surprising

Doesn't seem like there is anything to discuss in
this moment

It is now a week later and I still feel like there is nothing to discuss. None of any of the other projects I wrote about in the book are any closer to happening. But I honestly don't care.

I am sitting on the floor typing this while Henry is a few feet away, lying on our bed, happily watching some comedy special. A few moments ago, I left the living room, where Kate was reading on the couch, and walked down the hall past Eve in the other bedroom, laughing on the phone, talking to a friend. I still feel like I have everything I need and there is nothing else that I want.

And, of course, it has occurred to me that I was judging Glenn. So now that I am trying to stop judging people, I have no real feelings about Glenn. So in the end, I don't have any grudge against Glenn Close, not really.

YET ANOTHER AFTERWORD

JANUARY 29, 2024

Last night, we watched *Heartburn*. It's actually the second time I've watched it in the last six months, and maybe the third time I've watched it in the last year. I wish I had a job curating a *Heartburn* streaming service where I just programmed movies like *Heartburn*, even though nothing is really like *Heartburn*.

I was thinking about it this morning and realized, like *The Way We Were* and *Private Benjamin*, *Heartburn* has one of my favorite types of endings a movie can have. (If you don't want to know the ending of those movies, go to the next paragraph.) It's when someone, most often or maybe only a woman for some reason, says "Enough" and gets out of a bad situation and walks alone toward a better future. In *Heartburn*, she does it with two little children, but it still works. Just like it did when I walked onto the airplane bound for New York on July 8, 2022, with Kate and Henry and Eve.

Enough, I said as we all moved to New York.

And that's where we all are now. I was actually supposed to be in Minneapolis today for a volleyball tournament with Eve. I was all set to leave yesterday afternoon when Kate came into our bedroom and announced she had just hung up with Eve, who was at school.

"Everything is fine," she said, which is what she always says when everything isn't quite fine, but isn't as bad as it could be.

"What is it?" I asked nervously.

She explained that Eve had a slight concussion from volleyball practice the previous night. The doctors said she shouldn't go to the tournament, and so, magically, I am not in Minneapolis today.

Which is all to say, I thought I would be on the floor of a large convention center in the middle of the country when writing this afterword telling you where everyone ended up after the book ended, but instead I am on the floor of our apartment in New York. So you never know where you are going to end up describing where everyone ended up. Which can be thought of as upsetting, but in this moment, I consider it hopeful. After all, I was supposed to be in Minneapolis and now I'm not.

My friend Michelle was once married to man named Matt. He said something that always stayed with me.

"*The Wizard of Oz* has all the answers," he said. "If you have any question, *The Wizard of Oz* can answer it."

The main answer as we all know is: "There's no place like home." If you take that on the surface level, it is a homily. But if you are looking for answers, then it is profound. Home is the answer. You can look for answers outside of yourself or your home, but really you or your home is the answer.

And that is what this experience taught me. In my opinion, life teaches us what we need to learn. It is just up to us to figure out what it is that we need to learn.

Now, all these months and months later, it is hard for me to remember how the things I wrote about in the book ended. Most of them didn't just end, they faded away, but like in *American Graffiti* and many other movies, here is what happened to some of the people mentioned in the book:

Glenn. I never spoke to or heard from her again.

Pete. His show came on and no one I know watched it.

Amy Schumer. I did end up getting a job offer for the second season of *Life & Beth*. I tried to say yes, but I couldn't bring myself to actually do it. First, I asked for one more day to think about it. Then another. Then another. Finally, my lawyer called me and said, "Bruce, if you don't respond to their offer today, then that is basically a pass."

"Patti," I said. "I'm on the floor of my bathroom. I have chills and diarrhea. I took a COVID test, but it's not COVID. I just can't make myself take this job. I keep telling everyone that I don't like this show. I can't take a job on a show I hate. The show is Amy's baby and she loves it and all the writers in the room should love it. If you take the job and don't love the show, that is not fair to the creator."

"Then don't take the show," she said.

So I didn't.

The next day, I called Rob at CAA to explain. "I wanted to take the job," I said. "But my body rebelled."

"I heard," he said dryly. But after we talked it out, he seemed to have an understanding of why I did what I did. Or why I didn't do what I didn't do.

Kate Berlant and John Early. Kate and John just sort of stopped reaching out to me. At one point, Laura texted me, asking if I was still interested in their show. I texted back that I was interested if they were still interested in me. And then I never heard anything from anyone again. Oh wait, John texted me an invite to a show of a friend of his, which I couldn't make. I texted back:

I saw your name and was sure the text was Kate is in a coma come to the hospital ASAP

Then:

That is how my brain is wired.

Which it really is. This is what I meant about going to the darkest possible place at lightning speed. So imagine what it is like to be me getting texts. Before I read them. I live in fear always.

Andrew Singer. *Gilligan's Island* went away again, then came back. It actually had a meaningful step forward where I met with Universal and was ready to have a meeting with Peacock, but then there was a writers' strike and then, after the strike was over, Andrew texted that we could forget about *Gilligan's Island* for good. A few weeks ago, Andrew texted:

What about doing Gilligans as a Broadway musical? It might give us permission to keep it nostalgic, campy, and light.

I texted back:

Sounds great.

And never heard another word. Guess I will see you guys on Broadway.

Will Forte. His show with the Obamas hasn't come on yet, but I am sure it will be great.

The man at the gym whose phone I took. I have been back to Los Angeles since the book ended and went to the gym here and there. I saw him. We saw each other, and although we didn't talk, I know he hasn't forgotten what I did and he hasn't forgiven me.

Hamilton Leithauser. He wasn't in the book, but he is in the ending to the book. On one of my flights to Los Angeles, I watched the last episode of *The Last Movie Stars*, the Ethan Hawke documentary about Paul Newman and Joanne Woodward.

In the final moments of the final episode, there is a song by Hamilton Leithauser called "In Our Time." After it ended, I just rewound and watched the ending. Then watched it again.

And again. I can't quite explain why. But one reason might be this lyric:

Today is a day that we're starting again.

There is something that is both awful and amazing about that to me. Today is a day that we are starting again. So let's do it. Let's start again.

ACKNOWLEDGMENTS

You would not be reading this book, except for the fact that one magical day I received a phone call from two agents at UTA, Gregory McKnight and Dan Erlij. I told them about the book, which they read and then gave to Christy Fletcher, a book agent at UTA. Christy sent it to some editors, and Serena Jones at Henry Holt wanted to buy it. I am so grateful to these four people that I cannot even begin to express how grateful I am. Oh, I also want to thank Zoë Affron at Henry Holt, who magically guided me through the editorial process. Zoë, thank you again and again.

I also have to make a special thank you to Rob and Laura at CAA for being such indefatigable and joyful people and for being such good sports and kind souls.

This book began with Kate, Henry, and Eve and has to end with them. They are everything in the world to me, and I hope they know it even when I don't know it.

ABOUT THE AUTHOR

Bruce Eric Kaplan is a television writer and producer and a cartoonist for the *New Yorker*, among
other publications.